FIRST LADIES, CAN WE TALK?

Walking in Your Calling and Purpose

LEISA WYNN-JOHNSON

Largo, MD

Copyright © 2023 Leisa Wynn-Johnson

All rights reserved under the international copyright law. No part of this book may be reproduced or transmitted in any form or by any means, electronic or mechanical, including photocopying, recording, or by any information storage and retrieval system, without the express, written permission of the publisher or the author. The exception is reviewers, who may quote brief passages in a review.

Christian Living Books, Inc.
christianlivingbooks.com
We bring your dreams to fruition.

ISBN 9781562295837

Unless otherwise noted, Scripture quotations are taken from the King James Version of the Bible. Scripture quotations marked (AMP) are taken from the Amplified® Bible, Copyright © 2015 by The Lockman Foundation. Scripture quotations marked (ESV) are taken from The Holy Bible, English Standard Version®, Copyright © 2001 by Crossway, a publishing ministry of Good News Publishers. Scripture quotations marked (GNTD) are taken from the Good News Bible © 1994 published by the British and Foreign Bible Society. Good News Bible © American Bible Society 1966, 1971, 1976, 1992. Scripture quotations marked (NIV) are taken from the New International Version®, Copyright © 1973, 1978, 1984, 2011 by Biblica, Inc.® Used by permission of Zondervan. Scripture quotations marked (NKJV) are taken from the New King James Version, Copyright © 1982 by Thomas Nelson, Inc. Scripture quotations marked (TLB) are taken from The Living Bible Copyright © 1971. Used by permission of Tyndale House Publishers. All rights reserved.

ENDORSEMENTS

Lady Leisa speaks candidly about her journey as a Pastor's wife. The integration of Biblical principles and the author's personal narrative is a refreshing and inspiring read. The authenticity of Lady Johnson's experiences gives a voice to the countless women who are navigating through the complexities of their calling to serve alongside their husbands in this role. First Ladies are not alone in their journey and their feelings are deeply understood by their sisters who share this experience in the Kingdom of God. The author's insight and wisdom are a gift to Pastors and their wives.

— **Dr. Barbara McCoo Lewis**
General Supervisor, International Department of Women
Church of God in Christ, Inc.

Lady Leisa is a devoted wife and mother, and even more than that, she is a devoted minister. When I say "minister," I am not only referring to her competency in handling the Word of God. I am also alluding to her approach to effectively meeting the needs of others, whether through prayer, preaching, counseling, or being a visible, yet quiet presence for people. She executes each aspect with integrity, excellence, and compassion. It is because of these qualities that I am excited about this published work. This body of work has taken years of research and experience, and now you will be a recipient of her invaluable lessons. These lessons will help you navigate through your own ministry spaces as you discover your *what*, *why*, and *how* in ministry. Many times, knowing *what* is not enough motivation to continue moving forward. It must be accompanied by *why;* why is a critical foundational principle that encourages you to stay the course and keep going when ministry becomes overwhelming and seemingly impossible. Your *what* and *why* must also be accompanied by your *how*, which provides the practical tools needed to execute your ministry with intention. Leisa's writing brings these aspects together beautifully and succinctly in an easily applicable way.

— **DeSean Horne, M.Div.**
Pastor, Second Baptist Church, Reno, NV
Vice President, NV/CA Interstate Baptist Convention
Administrative Board Member, National Baptist Convention USA, Inc.

What a phenomenal, insightful, and necessary read for all First Ladies or ladies aspiring to be First Ladies! This book is poignant with a vivid flow! I am in awe of you, my sister! You will be better for reading *First Ladies, Can We Talk?*

— **Pastor Robbye Wynn Nicholson, MAPC**
Kingdom City Worship Center, Houston, TX

First Ladies, Can We Talk? The title alone grabs at your heart. I pray that each woman reading this book will see themselves in the pages. I encourage you to live and know that you are valuable. I encourage women to find a mother who they can glean from and sit at her feet. Congratulations to Lady Leisa for sharing the truth that will be encourage any woman reading. No matter what you face in your life, your purpose will not change.

— **Lady Vanessa W. Macklin**
Glad Tidings International Church of God in Christ, Hayward, CA

My dear friend, Lady Leisa, has been chosen by God to minister hope and healing to First Ladies throughout the world. Through her captivating book, *First Ladies, Can We Talk?* she has effectively provided an in-depth look into the many challenges and victories commonly faced by First Ladies. Yet, Lady Leisa offers words of comfort, hope, and empowerment for every challenge faced. I highly recommend this book, not only as a source of encouragement for First Ladies but as an insightful motivation for lay members everywhere to bombard heaven on behalf of their First Ladies.

— **Lady Elizabeth Rhone**
Mt. Sinai Church of God in Christ, Pomona CA
First Lady, Brazil Jurisdiction
Facilitator, Clergy Wives Prayer and Support Line

DEDICATION

I dedicate this book to every First Lady/Elect Lady and every woman on a journey of learning and growing. I pray you will embrace your journey with fortitude. Remember, you are not in this alone. You were created for this before the foundation of the world.

> I can do all things through Christ who strengthens me. (Philippians 4:13)

I also pray that you walk into your purpose with power and authority.

To MJ, I wrote this book for you. With humility, you wore pressure like a coat because you thought the way you loved God's people they would, in return, love you.

> Unto the pure all things are pure.
> (Titus 1:15a)

FOREWORD

First Ladies, can we talk? It is my prayer that First Ladies around the world will be open to receive what is so gracefully and passionately written in this book. You may not be a First Lady, but you are a woman, and you will also find yourself in some of these chapters. Life is filled with swift transitions, lessons, tests, trials, and pain, but the beauty and laughter produce the triumph that comes after. Lady Leisa has candidly and purposefully written this book to give you insight into the life of a First Lady her perspective and experiences.

As you read this book, I pray you will find the time to look at the parallels to what you may have experienced on your journey. Women come from all walks of life; we are diverse, and we all have our own experiences. Your story may not be Lady Leisa's story. Or perhaps it is. Whether it is or not, you too have a life-changing story.

In this unique book, you will read the stories of women and gain strategic insights from their experiences. You will see the vulnerability in trying to live victorious and free while loaded with commitments, even showing up when faced with painful and disheartening situations. The goal of this book is to help you reprogram your thoughts and harness your emotions to respond appropriately and intelligently without reacting. Wisdom is the principal thing.

Women must learn to respond and not react! Yes, our emotions are God-given. But the way we learn to handle them determines our outcomes—good or bad—when dealing with insecurity, marriage, regret, shame, condemnation, responsibility, vulnerability, the truth, children, the saints, and, most importantly, ourselves.

This beautifully written book of examples, stories, and first-hand observations will help you to explore the depths of your thought processes and your heart when emotions are raging. The fight for life is huge, and the Enemy will present continuous scenarios of drama. First Ladies, can we talk? With deep reflection, Lady Leisa invites you to have a seat as she shares her life up close and personal, so you can learn from her experiences.

First Ladies, my sisters, I have an awesome responsibility in writing the foreword of this book. I asked Lady Leisa, "Why are you writing this book now?" Her response was, "Because I care for women. I want them to be confident, know their purpose, and find some things they love to do. I desire that women see their value and know they have something important to bring to any ministry and any table. I want women to know their voices are powerful, and they are second-class citizens to no one."

Lady Leisa goes on to say, "This book is not to be viewed as a badge of negativity. Rather, it has a positive outlook on how you can become better than you have ever imagined in your walk with the Lord and your life as a woman." And I concur! We all have a past, and by the grace of God, we are going somewhere to be a blessing to that woman who is stuck, to that woman who has sunk, to that woman who is depressed, to that woman who feels alone, to that woman who is having trouble finding her purpose, and to that woman who is struggling to balance life. We tell you, "Woman, rise up and be great!"

As you read this book, if you find yourself in the pages, embrace the reality; dissect it; take a moment to pause, and pray as you reflect on your own journey.

I speak to women everywhere, and I decree and declare your future has promise, and your victory is assured! Make sound adjustments; stand in your truth fairly; keep your mouth moving and keep talking to God. Ask God to help you to see yourself as bold and forthright. Lady Leisa is transparent and authentic with her stories. I'm sure there were moments when she experienced depression, indecisiveness, uncertainty, and anxiety… but she still had to be accountable to God, her family, and the man of God, her husband. She still had to be there for the people. That's tough for anyone! This book will light the way for you too.

At times, people will not understand your obedience and allegiance to God, but you must know who you are serving and who God is to you in your convictions.

I firmly believe it would be very useful to take notes as this book describes how women are seen from Leisa's perspective. It is definitely empowering. Take note, women, the First Lady can be a team player, and she can also be a destroyer. It is vitally important that a woman knows when to speak and how to speak: tone, cadence, and volume contribute to the success of an event… and in her home life.

Foreword

Congratulations to Lady Leisa! You have written a book with layers of information, examples in the Word of God, vulnerability, and authenticity for the reader to grow and gain helpful insights. You have given the reader truth from your perspective. I challenge and encourage every woman to share the conversations of a woman who sees you and loves you together with other women without judgment. We soar, we learn, and we do better together. Thank You, Father, for a timely book that will catapult, transform, and give clarity to women across the globe.

— **Lady Vicki Kemp**
Greater Harvest Christian Center, Bakersfield, CA
Bestselling author of *Better Than Yesterday, Grace in Deep Waters,*
and *Early Will I Seek Thee*

CONTENTS

Introduction	13
The Death of the King	17
When Doves Cry	23
Vent Up	37
Grace	49
My Hubby, My Lover, My Friend	59
Who Am I?	73
When the Bough Breaks	85
What About the Children?	93
First Ladies Speak	101
Wife of the Pastor or the Pastor's Wife?	111
Conclusion	123
Acknowledgments	129
About the Author	131

INTRODUCTION

We play so many roles as First Ladies. The shoes in this book represent those different roles and the various paths we take to function in those roles. Of course, I would be remiss if I didn't let you in on a little secret… I love me some pumps. The images of shoes are also a fun way to represent the various walks of life from which we hail and is symbolic of my subtitle *Walking in Your Calling and Purpose.*

I was asked whether our role as First Ladies a calling is and I replied, "When God created Eve for Adam. He said, 'It is not good for man to be alone; I will make a help meet for him.'" This is found in Genesis 2:18 and it means "I will make him a woman who is suitable for him." "To be called" in the Greek means "invited," and "summoned." It means "to serve." You have been invited to serve. My dear First Lady, I want this book to encourage you to strive for what God wants you to be, for you have indeed been chosen. Congratulations! You have been called! Embrace your calling.

I wrote this book for the ones who understand being a First Lady is not a call to fame or popularity; this is a call to sacrifice—to live a consecrated life offered up to God.

> I beseech you therefore brethren by the mercies of God to present your bodies a living sacrifice, holy acceptable unto God which is your reasonable service.
>
> (Romans 12:1)

I wrote this book to salute the pastors' wives of old who endured it all at a time when pastors' wives were just fixtures in the church. They worked hard to pave the way for us today. They taught us the importance of having a relationship with God. They taught us that without the anchor of a home, we can do nothing. They taught us to pray for our husbands, even when situations arise that have nothing to do with us because we are all in this together. You might not be able to sing a single note, but we have all been called to prayer. Prayer is our weapon against the wiles and tricks of the wicked one.

I also wrote this book for the First Lady lovingly called the "elect lady," who enjoys her role, who is immersed in the Word and has a comfortable place that is well-suited to her. However, this book will help every woman. Whether you are a First Lady or not, it will inspire you in many areas of your life.

First Ladies, can we talk? I see you smile in the face of negative comments and criticism. I see you keeping the balance and poise of the ministry. You are the example people long for. You work well with your husband. You are a team player. Girl, you have learned to "share" the man of God with the people, while you guard his heart and your mind. You are a phenomenal woman!

I wrote this to the intercessor in you. I see you praying and asking God for direction because more than anything, you would never want to let the Lord down. This book is for those of you who walk in that position, those who will be in the position, and for the elect lady who is wondering whether there is a place for you. I say to you all, your experience will help other First Ladies who will make their journeys. I pray this book blesses all of you.

My Affirmation to All Women

Women, I affirm that you are beautiful and powerful, and you deserve God's best for your lives. You are gifts to the world and God is with you always, even in stormy weather. I affirm that every need in your life is met. In the name of Jesus. I pray that you will know who you are in the kingdom. I pray you will look through the eyes of faith and affirm that you are God's daughter.

After each chapter, I encourage you to write your own affirmation in the space provided for you. Affirm the results you would like to see happen in your own life. Jesus did not pray for the challenges, drama, and situations He was facing. Rather, He prayed for the results. May you have great success and victory in your life.

Love,

Lady Leisa Wynn-Johnson

*Make this book your own.
Add a lovely picture of yourself
and see yourself in the
pages of this book.*

THE DEATH OF THE KING

In the year that King Uzziah died, I saw the Lord sitting on a throne, high and lifted up, and the train of His robe filled the temple.
(Isaiah 6:1 NKJV)

King Uzziah represented the stability of Judah. History remembers him as an efficient administrator and military leader under whose leadership his subjects gained many things. The year of his death marked a significant change in the natural order of the kingdom, but it also had profound spiritual implications. That was the year the prophet Isaiah received his call to preach the word to the nations.

I had the same experience when my husband's beloved father, Pastor Harold Johnson, Sr., passed away in 2005. In my eyes, my life seemed normal. My priorities consisted of seeing to the well-being of my family—cooking, cleaning, maintaining our home, and all the other duties associated with being a wife and mother. My husband was the lead musician at the church and played for the choir and during the sermon. We were happy and content serving in the church and never discussed the possibility of him becoming a pastor. We were faithful and obedient as we went about our weekly tasks of cleaning the church—from shining the brass at the top of the stairs to vacuuming and dusting the furniture.

My husband and I trained our children to clean the temple of God without complaining. We would say things like, "It is a privilege to do this job." Often, I would think about the Levites and how they ministered in the tabernacle. When Moses came down from Mt. Sinai, while the children of Israel were worshiping the golden calf, the only tribe that did not participate was the tribe of Levi:

> For they [the Levites] are wholly given over to me from among the children of Israel. (Numbers 8:16a NKJV)

I had no idea that the house of God we loved and cared for would one day become the church my husband now pastors. I am often reminded of this passage of Scripture:

> And if you have not been faithful in that which belongs to another man's who shall give you what is your own?
> (Luke 16:12 NKJV)

In our denomination, the bishop selects the next pastor as the successor when the current pastor dies. So, when our pastor died, we were told a selection would be made. I didn't think it would be us! Truthfully, I prayed it wouldn't be us (laugh out loud!). After the passing of my father-in-law, my husband and I had discussed moving to Las Vegas. We decided we would move away after one year of helping the new pastor transition. My husband would evangelize and help the church settle. I was fine with moving. Can you hear me, sisters? First Ladies?

Familiar Territory

In October 2005, my life changed forever. I remember that night as if it was yesterday. It was a nice, mildly warm night—no coats. Yet, when we walked into the church, I could feel the sudden, frigid, and cold demeanor of the people who we worshiped with, laughed with, and talked to on a regular basis. Unbeknownst to me, the people had already taken sides. Lord, have mercy!

You see, this was an unfamiliar feeling to my husband, but for me, there was this overwhelming feeling of impertinence that I knew all too well. This was the exact feeling that I had as a young woman when my eight siblings and I were at a meeting at the church where my father, the Late Reverend Willie J. Wynn pastored. We were waiting to hear the announcement of who my father's successor was going to be. This meeting took place only 30 days after the passing of my father.

My father was a man of great honor. He was such a wonderful father and great husband to my dear mother. He was an example to the world! When we lost him, we were devastated, and the feelings of grief were unexplainable. I remember my mom, siblings, and I sat on the front pew, and all I could think about was my father and who

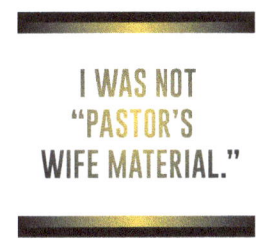

could possibly replace him and fill his shoes. That same knot was in my stomach! But I didn't know why. My husband and I hadn't said anything to the bishop; we were just there to support whoever he chose. After all, I was not "pastor's wife material" since I was mouthy and opinionated, but I loved God's people, right?

The whole congregation was in attendance. As the bishop mounted the podium, the room pulsated with a sense of anticipation. I knew that most of the congregation already had their minds fixed on who they thought should be the next pastor of this prominent church that was built by their late pastor. The edifice was a massive, beautiful building with mauve and gold accents, upholstered pews, brass railings that lined the upstairs balcony, and a gold cross mounted on the back wall of the pulpit. The sanctuary alone could seat 1,000 or more! We all waited anxiously as the bishop said his preliminaries and the whole time, I was saying to myself, "Vegas, here we come!" because surely, it wouldn't be my husband! After all, he had only been walking in his "Christian faith" for ten years, while the other candidates had been serving God and working in ministry much longer.

What Just Happened?

The bishop cleared his throat. You could hear a pin drop on the hardwood floor! And then he proceeded to say, "The next pastor of Old Path Church will be Pastor Harold Johnson, Jr." I immediately felt the blood rush from my head, down to my feet as a million emotions flooded my mind. My husband was sitting in the front pew of the church, along with his mother and his sisters. I remember looking at him from across the room, but he wouldn't make eye contact with me. I needed him to look at me! I desperately needed him to tell me I was dreaming and that they had called the wrong name. To my surprise and dismay, he never looked at me once, not

First Ladies, Can We Talk?

even acknowledging me with a nod in my direction. Couldn't he feel that I needed him? Little did I know, he needed me just as much!

As I began to look over the church, everything seemed to be moving in slow motion. I watched as my friends—or so-called friends—the ladies I went to lunch with, attended baby showers and birthday parties with, and kept in frequent contact with, became apprehensive as they looked in my direction with their faces filled with disappointment and disbelief. At that very moment, six families got up and walked out the door. I kept saying to myself, "What just happened?"

In one moment, my life changed—without my consent. After the bishop made his announcement, he called my husband and me up to the podium. I could not move. Even though I kept telling my feet to move, they would not! I was holding my youngest son on my lap, and I remember thinking to myself, "There must be some kind of a mistake. This cannot be happening. Not me! I'm not ready. I will have to change too much, and I'm afraid I will lose myself trying."

Finally, someone came and got my son from me. Once I was able to move my legs and make it to the podium, I looked at the faces of those who were still there. I said a few words, but no one in the audience made eye contact with me. When I was finished, I took my seat on the side of the church where I always sat. I looked up at my husband, standing tall at 6'3", apparently unshaken by what had just occurred. I realized at that moment our lives were not ours anymore. He answered the call without question or doubt. I also began my journey but not without much anxiety.

PRAYER

Lord, I pray that my sisters and First Ladies everywhere learn to love as You declare we should in the Word of God. Give us an understanding and feel for each other's heartbeat. In the seasons when life gives us a big sucker punch, I pray that as women of God, we would be understanding and not judgmental. Lord, help us to look to You rather than our emotions.

We will trust You in everything we encounter. In times of death, pain, uncertainty, and yes even in divorce, we will look to the cross and be sensitive to those around us. Dear Lord, help us to be what You have called us to be. We were hand-picked by You to walk alongside the man of God, Your servant. Help us to hear Your voice clearly as we walk in this God-given role daily. See our hearts and intentions as we strive to always do things Your way. In Jesus' name. Amen.

WRITE YOUR AFFIRMATION OF OBEDIENCE

_____
_____
_____
_____
_____
_____
_____
_____

CHAPTER 2

WHEN DOVES CRY

> Hear my prayer, O Lord, and let my cry come unto thee. Hide not thy face from me in the day when I am in trouble; incline thine ear unto me: in the day when I call answer me speedily. (Psalm 102:1-2)

A few years ago, I was having a conversation with another First Lady when she instructed me to "learn the demeanor of the dove." The dove produces a soft drawn-out coo or call that mimics the sound of a lamenting cry. I was unaware that there would be so many days that I would have to lament. As elect ladies, we possess this cry or passionate expression. It is a cry that only we can hear and truly understand.

In 2006, I met an elect lady (I will call her Pearl) who was much older than I was. She was about 5'3", small in stature with beautiful skin. Her church was not only a growing church but a thriving ministry. As an elect lady, Pearl had the experience, the know-how, and the look! She was a classy dresser and well-put-together. During the first night of my Sister-2-Sister Conference, she helped pray for people and became a great supporter of this annual event.

However, I sensed something was wrong, but I could not put my finger on it. Pearl walked over to me during the last night of the conference and said, "Hey, Lady, when you write your book, make sure you write about when doves cry."

"Why?" I asked.

She replied, "Only a dove can hear the cry of another dove."

I smiled and, as she walked away, I noticed her sadness but did not address it at that time. As the "new kid on the block," who was I and how could I help? I had no idea that a few years later, she would take her own life.

I know this assignment can get hard and rough and there will be times when you want to throw in the towel and tell everyone you could be doing something else. But I say to you, my sister (yes, you are my sister), be encouraged; hold on; cry if you must—that's part of it. As the old folks used to say, "Trouble doesn't last always," and "This too shall pass." There have been days I questioned God, "Are You sure You want me?" Whenever I am in doubt, I always find my answer in God's Word, and He says, "Be still, and know that I am God" (Psalm 46:10).

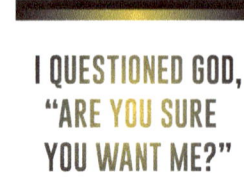

I QUESTIONED GOD, "ARE YOU SURE YOU WANT ME?"

Being still means to stop striving, relax, and stop fighting. First Ladies, God gives us the grace to stand with our husbands. This is a calling and if you're not equipped, it will destroy you or you will destroy it. You are the one God chose! Be the best you can be in Him.

Elect ladies come in many different varieties. From my observations over the years, here's how some can be characterized.

THE CHURCH MOUSE

She's quiet. Her husband is less apt to ask for her assistance because he wants her to focus on child rearing and their home life. Therefore, her primary ministry is to the man of God and their family. In some cases, the church mouse has learned to survive by keeping herself busy with friends and family. However, her true calling and ministry must remain on hold while she prays for things to change for her.

You would never know if this elect lady was happy or not unless she told you. I knew an elect lady who was on the usher board at her church and seemed to be satisfied with that position.

Another elect lady was fine with just sitting in the pews on the far side of the church with the children and no one noticed them. If you visited their church, she just blended in with everyone else. Whether this dynamic was right or wrong, I cannot say. However, if this works for them without breaking their spirits, then so be it. Let me encourage you—you are an important, valuable woman—never let anyone say differently. Peace is your portion:

> If it is possible, as far as it depends on you, live at peace with everyone. (Romans 12:18 NIV)

THE ANT

She is a hard worker who goes above and beyond her obligations to her husband. She seldom makes her feelings known no matter how exhausted or in need she may be. She never says no and just does it (whatever "it" may be) for the sake of the ministry. Some would say she's a little overworked.

The ant is wise, hard-working, and knows her place. She is also detailed, industrious, prudent, and knows how to get the job done. The spirit of excellence resides in her. In addition to the ministry, she has alongside her husband, she recognizes God's call on her life as well. This call is acknowledged by her husband. He allows her to operate and enjoy her ministry because he knows she is a gift to the body of Christ.

The ant flourishes both in the church and in the marketplace because of her favorable environment. Indeed, she is praised as a role model:

> Go to the ant thou sluggard; consider her ways and be wise.
> (Proverbs 6:6)

The ant knows what to do without guidance but with instinct. *Gill's Exposition of the Entire Bible* writes of Proverbs 6:7: "Which having no guide, overseer, or ruler. None to guide and direct her on what to do, nor any to overlook her to see what she does right or oblige her to work and keep her to an account. The ant is industrious."

Remember, this is not a position where you should neglect yourself. First Ladies must learn to come up for air and practice self-care.

THE CONTROLLER

She sits back and watches. If she is a good controller, you never see her coming. This elect lady has usually been with her husband/pastor from the beginning. Her blood, sweat, and tears are as much a part of the ministry as her husband's. Things were not always this good. However, due to great sacrifices and going without in the family, and because of much prayer and hard work, the circumstances have changed for the better.

She sees to it that everything runs well and wants to underplay "the controller" title but it is a fact. Remember, she means no harm, but people and circumstances have helped develop her into who she is. Therefore, I must give the controller some slack because protecting her husband's heart is her priority as she watches people come and go in the ministry. In all that, no one ever sees her battle scars or patches her wounds.

The fact is, who this First Lady really is and who we actually see are two very different people. The controller must wear many hats while supporting her husband as he excels and advances in the ministry. This is not the spirit of pride as much as a feeling of sincere gratitude. For this reason, the controller is often misunderstood. However, before you pass judgment, I say walk a mile in her shoes. This elect lady loves the Lord; she never puts herself before her husband in word or deed. We pray for her—we hear her cry:

> The righteous cry out, and the LORD hears, and delivers them out of all their troubles. (Psalm 34:17 NKJV)

THE EXPERT

She is by no means a novice; she's a very intelligent and seasoned person. Although she grew up in a ministry pastored by her parents, she has one of her own. The expert often takes the back seat on purpose, so it does not look as if she is trying to run the ministry. This First Lady encourages and supports her husband, even when she doesn't understand him. She would never disrespect him although she knows exactly what to do and how much she could help him. She often laments due to her knowledge and expertise of how to do things versus how much she is allowed to assist. Whether it is working in the community or the church, God commands blessings upon everything this First Lady sets her hands to do. Her only motive and heart's desire is to glorify and please the Lord in every aspect of her life.

The expert may tend to be devalued in her local church because she moves with a God kind of confidence. As a result, everyone's expectations of her are great. However, she can only really help when she is asked, and her main objective is to help her husband and the church in an unassuming manner. Due to her solid and effective prayer life, this First Lady is called upon by other ministries for advice and counsel. Even though this constant shift between her real abilities and her prescribed role can be both harmful and dangerous, the expert will not abandon ship. Instead, she will continue to pray because she believes in the God of the Bible:

> My soul, wait thou only on you God; for my expectation is from him. (Psalm 62:5)

At times, this elect lady encounters disrespect because of her strong and assertive personality. In addition, other pastors may feel she could be a threat by causing to their wives to become more talkative or opinionated. However, the expert is a woman of wisdom who would never intentionally disappoint or embarrass her husband because it is important to her that he shines, and that the will of God is done in his life. She stays because she knows the God they both serve is at work in her husband and will show him who his wife is called and anointed to be in the ministry.

I have witnessed firsthand how the Devil tries to work in this situation because he knows how much the ministry would flourish if this First Lady's husband/pastor would release her to operate freely in her gifting. However, many elect ladies have to deal with the culture of their churches, where they are expected to just sit pretty and not get involved. Nonetheless, this pastor's wife has worked alongside her husband in every aspect related to the church. As a result of her patient labor in the Lord, the expert can wait patiently for her ministry to go forth. Delay does not mean denial.

THE SHELL WALKER

Have you ever visited a church where the elect lady's frustration can be observed? Even though she is available and could be an asset to her husband's ministry, she's often overlooked and thought of last.

We have an event in our denomination called the Pastor and Wife's Appreciation. I have attended some of these events where the majority of the church membership only speaks well of the pastor, while his wife sits there silently, smiling as though her heart isn't working. To maintain peace at any cost, in wisdom, this elect lady acts as if she has done nothing in the ministry. The shell walker does not want to draw attention to herself, so she remains sweet, quiet, and respectful.

My heart goes out to this elect lady more than all the others because her silence comes through stronger than her words could ever say. I pray for her, and I also salute her. I don't judge her. I refuse judgment. No one knows what they would do if they were in her shoes. What do you think? She must navigate the slippery slope that is her husband's invidiousness. She constantly feeds his ego and assures him of his greatness to keep the peace. Remember that wisdom is always your best friend.

These First Ladies walk on eggshells without shoes and do not make a sound. I call this mental and emotional tension "Psychological Warfare." Psychological warfare involves actions intended to reduce the opponents' morale, keep them underfoot, and under surveillance when you are nowhere around. I saw this when I worked at the prison. A man is sentenced to life, but a woman living outside the gates who could drive or live anywhere she wants is psychologically tied to this man behind bars. He tells her what she can and cannot do. Meanwhile, she forgets that he cannot do anything to her because he's not getting out of prison!

I pray for these elect ladies who are walking on shells and ask God to show them what to do.

THE TEAM PLAYER

She is the Serita to his Jakes, the Michelle to his Barack. Together, they are the power couple. He has a vision and she, as his elect-lady, helps him make it happen. His vision becomes her vision; his goals become hers. No inhibitions, no secrets, just harmony for the sake of the cause. This First Lady is fulfilled by helping and supporting her husband/pastor.

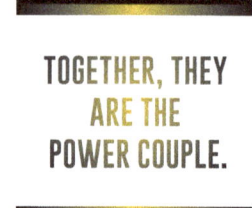

TOGETHER, THEY ARE THE POWER COUPLE.

When I was a young girl, I observed my mom and dad's interactions. My dad never asked my mom to do anything that made her uncomfortable. One time when they needed something done at the church, he sent her over because he was confident, she could meet the need due to her pleasant personality.

The team player is not just there to make her husband look good but to make them both look good. She is there to complement the things God is asking him to do. Sometimes the team player will be a combination of critic and best passive asset, and the two work well together. However, it does not mean they do not disagree. We will never know if Serita Jakes ever disagrees with Bishop Jakes. What we will see is his biggest cheerleader clapping, standing in honor, and performing any other gestures necessary to support him. First Ladies, the world will criticize and beat down our husbands/pastors. Therefore, it is our job to lift them up, patch every cut, and give them the boost they need to go forward fighting the good fight of faith yet another day.

THE DOLL

The China doll is made from fine, glazed porcelain material from which it derives its name. According to the *Encyclopedia Britannica*, porcelain is vitrified pottery with a white fine-grained body that is usually translucent.

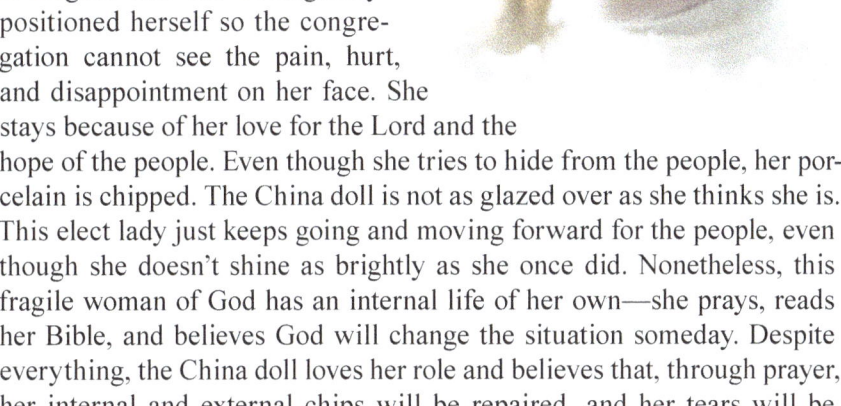

Symbolically, the China doll is fragile. She has strategically positioned herself so the congregation cannot see the pain, hurt, and disappointment on her face. She stays because of her love for the Lord and the hope of the people. Even though she tries to hide from the people, her porcelain is chipped. The China doll is not as glazed over as she thinks she is. This elect lady just keeps going and moving forward for the people, even though she doesn't shine as brightly as she once did. Nonetheless, this fragile woman of God has an internal life of her own—she prays, reads her Bible, and believes God will change the situation someday. Despite everything, the China doll loves her role and believes that, through prayer, her internal and external chips will be repaired, and her tears will be wiped from her eyes. We see and salute you, China doll!

THE MIDWIFE

The midwife specializes in birthing and bringing forth spiritual children. In the natural birth process, there are four stages. When a mother goes into labor, the early stages of labor seem to be the longest stages. This is when the midwife assures you that your body is getting ready to give birth so get ready for the long-haul. Spiritually, the midwife instructs you to stay prayerful, keep reading your Bible, don't forget to fast, and other spiritual disciplines. When labor gets unbearable, she will help you to change positions to ease your pain.

The midwife is there to help you deliver what God is doing in your life and what God has called you to be. They know that after you have suffered a while, you've cried, and you have laughed a little, you will be ready to hear the midwife say, PUSH! You're ready to give birth. Your water has broken; you are crowning (they call this the ring of fire). You're almost there then she says again for the last time, PUSH! I've seen spiritual midwives help others birth what God had in store for them in ministry. This midwife is usually an older First Lady that is only doing for them what someone else did for her.

THE WARRIOR

Often, I am mistaken for a midwife. However, I know I am a warrior; that is one who specializes in spiritual warfare. Can you relate to what I am saying here? I know you can. Let us go deeper. I can position you to receive your help so you can break through your situations, trials, tribulations, heartaches, and heartbreaks. I permit you to be who you are and who God made you to be.

In this field (I am calling it that on purpose), who are you? Are you the warrior who will get down on your knees and help others in need pray through, reach God, and discover who they are in God? Once you help these individuals reach the point of breakthrough, you can have the midwives (elect ladies) nurture them step-by-step, precept upon precept, through the Word of God until they reach a place of maturity where they can stand on their own.

I can help lead you to God, but someone else has to walk with you along God's path for your life. I can give you instructions, but someone else must disciple you and teach you how to develop a personal relationship with the Lord. Someone else must encourage and instruct you on how to stay away from chronic or acute disconnections and provide the tools needed to stay and remain connected to the vine.

As First Ladies, we must primarily have a strong relationship with God, one that goes beyond church activities. There's no way you can deal with people and their proclivities and idiosyncrasies without your own personal relationship with God. You will find that you won't always say or even do the right things. But our goal is to know God for ourselves and always do our best to please Him, even though people discover things about us or bring things out of us.

I had a particular incident with a lady whom the warrior part of me helped to connect with God. She needed and wanted more from me, but I didn't have the resources to give her. We must learn we are not the be-all and end-all of people's needs. Do not be so insecure that you can't allow other women in your church or surroundings to help nurture these people. If that's not something you know how to do or are not good at, then be who you are, and don't try to be everything to everybody.

> **DON'T TRY TO BE EVERYTHING TO EVERYBODY.**

I was dealing with this lady, and to be honest, I didn't really care for her. She was rude, very condescending, and extremely pushy. I know my limitations—God knows them too—but she wanted a part of me that I could not give. Being raised as a pastor's child, I saw my parents sometimes give people what I thought should have been given to us—notably, their time and talent. That's why I decided I was not going to be a pastor's wife. This was something I neither wanted nor expected.

This lady pushed me to the very edge, and I have to be honest; God told me, "Don't bother that lady." But I did anyway. The lady was standing and talking with a mutual friend. I walked over to where they were and said to the lady in a very condescending way, "glad to see you!" because she hadn't been to church in a while, and I wanted to expose her unfaithfulness to our friend. In my flesh, I knew that was going to irritate her, and my spirit told me not to do so—but I overrode the Holy Spirit. The next thing I knew, she called my husband and told him that she felt disrespected by me.

She was a thorn in my flesh! Have you ever met someone who seems to like confrontation and is always negative, disagreeable, and disrespectful? Well, that was this lady. I know I didn't have to say anything to her that night, but I did! I didn't listen to the voice of the Lord, so I know I deserved His chastisement. I learned very quickly from that experience not to allow anyone to take me out of character, regardless of who is right. So, in order to do the right thing and please God, eventually, I had to go back to that lady with my tail tucked and apologize. When I did, I began to cry—not because I was wrong but because, if I had just obeyed God, I would not have been in that situation.

Authenticity

One thing I will tell you throughout this book is that people appreciate authenticity, and they can smell a fake a mile away. Don't let anyone change you. If you're quiet but spiritual, be who you are. If you're loud but spiritual, be that. Just be who God has made you to be. He's not asking you to be anyone else.

Even though we all have our differences, First Ladies are basically all the same. Praise comes to us easily when we are happy, and our life experiences are positive. Lamentation enters through the door of chaotic experiences, brokenness, death, vulnerability, and hurt. To see a scriptural difference between the two, read the following verses:

> But thou art holy, O thou that inhabitest the praises of Israel. (Psalm 22:3)
>
> Why standest thou afar off O Lord? Why hidest thou thyself in times of trouble? (Psalm 10:1 KJV)

Remember how the dove symbolizes peace and hope? It was released as a sign of life after the flood (Genesis 8:11). We too must walk in peace bringing hope along with us. That's why as elect ladies, we should be the instruments of peace, not confusion. We should avoid confrontation at all costs. We are who God says we are. We know He is holy, and this is our God-given assignment.

His Glory

I was asking God the other day about His glory when I heard the words of a song by Lady Karen Clark Sheard.

> *Show me Your glory.*
> *I want to gaze into the beauty of Your holiness.*
> *Show me Your glory.*
> *I'm desperate to see.*
> *I will be still as You reveal Your glory.*

I started to meditate on those words. The glory of God is His invisible presence manifesting visibly through my life, your life, and everything we do so that God gets the glory. The heavens declare the glory of God as expressed in this psalm:

When Doves Cry

> The heavens declare the glory of God; the skies proclaim
> the work of his hands. Day after day they pour forth speech;
> night after night they reveal knowledge. (Psalm 19:1 NIV)

I want to live in a manner that people don't see me but what they see is God's glory, God's grace, God's anointing, and God's love shining through me. One thing God will not share is His glory. As we walk through what we call life and what God has assigned us to do, we must be mindful of two things:

1. God put us here.
2. We all have different shoes to walk in.

We must also remember we're not doing this by ourselves. We have the greatest gift of all—the Holy Ghost, the Paraclete, walking alongside us. The Bible says He will bring things to our remembrance. We are not alone. We have God by our side through all the misunderstandings and negative feedback from people who do not like what is said or done.

Can we talk, First Lady? You were meant for this assignment. It has your name written all over it. No one does it better; no one can do it better. But you will notice throughout this book, I tell you that you must not look at other First Ladies and try to be like them. They are fulfilling the assignment in the way God needs it to be done for such a time as this. Be yourself and stir up the gifts that are inside of you! Be who God made you to be. You were not born into this role and maybe you did not desire it, but God chose you for this assignment at this time.

> **GOD CHOSE YOU FOR THIS ASSIGNMENT AT THIS TIME.**

So, whether you wear a big hat or jeans and pumps, your role is to complement your husband and look good by his side. Remember, prayer is your primary weapon. It equips you for a role you may not think you were prepared for or even take you places you may not want to go, but God has made you fit for the battle by equipping you. We're all in the same boat, so let's lift each other up and pray for one another.

When doves cry, I hear you and you hear me. I see you and you see me. You know when it's authentic and okay to talk to God in prayer. Never think you're doing this alone. God's got you! This is a unique place to be, elect lady, or whatever they call or tag you. God knows you're in the right place.

In I Samuel chapter 29, David and his men had a rude awakening when they returned to base camp in Ziklag. They found out that their wives and children had been taken captive by the enemy and their homes were burned. The men were so mad at David, they wanted to stone him. But David did something extraordinary; he "encouraged himself in the Lord." As he did so, the Lord gave him the strategy for victory. They went into the enemy's camp, defeated them, and rescued their wives and children.

We face similar trials in our role. There will be victories where people applaud you, tell you you've done great, and thank you for being by their pastor's side. Then there will be times the same people will cheer him and smile at him but won't even look your way. Always remember David and encourage yourself in the Lord.

This assignment was not meant for you to look great, especially if you're doing it the way God has told you. Don't break under the pressure. Walk it out day by day, asking God to lead and guide you to the best strategy. Never share your opinion with your critics. Tell them what the Bible says. Sometimes we think we must know all the answers, but it's always best to show them what God is saying in the situation. That way, if they want to argue with anybody, they will have to take it up with God. Although we are individuals, we are the same. I am the same as you; you are the same as me.

PRAYER

From the ends of the earth, I will cry to please You, Lord, and only You. In pleasing You, whatever needs to be done will be done, and whatever needs to be said will be said, seasoned with grace. I will acknowledge You in all I do, and I will keep Your name high and lifted up. I will declare and affirm Your Word in all that I speak. In Jesus' name. Amen.

WRITE YOUR AFFIRMATION OF ENCOURAGEMENT

_____
_____
_____
_____
_____
_____
_____
_____
_____
_____
_____

CHAPTER 3

VENT UP

> Do not let any unwholesome talk come out of your mouths, but only what is helpful for building others up according to their needs, that it may benefit those who listen. (Ephesians 4:29 NIV)

Growing up as a pastor's child, I knew when to keep my mouth shut and just listen. I soon realized that some people only wanted to be close to the first family's kids to get information about their parents or even harm their children. I fed off of the vibes of the church people and learned early to vent and confide in those who I believe understand me and have my best interest at heart.

What about you? Who is mentoring you? Are there godly women who are doing this ministry successfully? Everybody needs somebody to talk to and be open with. We all want someone we can trust and share what's in our hearts without judgment and repercussions. I was told long ago that only leaders vent. This implies that we must be careful with whom we confide in because you never know who your secrets might be shared with.

Have you ever put your foot in your mouth—including your big toe and your heel? Thinking before we talk first is such a scarce commodity. We don't know the negative impact we can have on someone when we do not have filters, and we speak without thinking. I have learned there are some people who want to get to know you just to be in the know, and some genuinely want to truly get know you. Ponder that.

So run from what I call "Drama."

D – Designed

R – Reproach

A – Against

M – My

A – Anointing

As a pastor's wife, you learn quickly when to speak up, when to engage in a conversation, and when to move on. Grammy Award winner Kenny Rogers wrote these compelling lyrics in his 1979 song "The Gambler":

You've got to know when to hold 'em,

Know when to fold 'em,

Know when to walk away,

Know when to run...

A pastor's wife once asked me to explain, "Why is it that people can share their views and how they feel, but if I do the same, it goes viral? Is there ever a safe place?" Not always, but you will learn quickly who to trust. I have seen some elect women vent and share their secrets indiscriminately, resulting in painful betrayals because of their words. Let me make myself very clear: not every First Lady can be trusted. Therefore, you must pray, pray, pray! Ask God for discernment about who you can talk to. When there seems to be no one, talk to Him. God has a listening ear and is waiting for you to talk to Him. A pastor's wife once said to me, "I don't know how people make it without God." Me neither—sometimes it's hard when you still feel the hurt, pain, and fear.

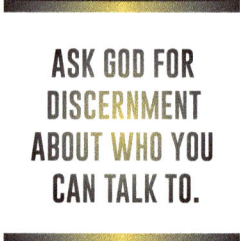

ASK GOD FOR DISCERNMENT ABOUT WHO YOU CAN TALK TO.

In the early part of our ministry when another First Lady and I attended a class for elect ladies, I was expecting help. Instead, we were told that if we had any problems, the problem was us. I left the class feeling bad and alone, wondering if I was the only one unsure of my responsibilities to God and my husband.

Gear Up

Surround yourself with constructive people who will tell you the truth without lecturing you and those who can direct you to help. Above all, don't leave home without wearing your spiritual armor. These six pieces of armor protect you from every device of Satan that targets your mind and body. The apostle Paul tells us:

> Finally, my brethren, be strong in the Lord, and in the power of his might. Put on the whole armor of God, that ye may be able to stand against the wiles of the devil. For we wrestle not against flesh and blood, but against principalities, against powers, against the rulers of the darkness of this world, against spiritual wickedness in high places. Wherefore take unto you the whole amour of God, that ye may be able to withstand in the evil day, and having done all, to stand. Stand therefore, having your loins girt about with truth, and having on the breastplate of righteousness; And your feet shod with the preparation of the gospel of peace; Above all, taking the shield of faith, wherewith ye shall be able to quench all the fiery darts of the wicked. And take the helmet of salvation, and the sword of the Spirit, which is the word of God. (Ephesians 6:10-17)

Wear your armor confidently. Gird your waist with the belt of truth, which is the Word of God.

> Thy word is a lamp unto my feet, and a light unto my path.
> (Psalm 119:105)

The Word will guide you constantly. The Enemy is banking on you not knowing the Word, so surprise him. Secure your breastplate around your chest. In our calling, we sustain so many major blows to our hearts because we don't wear our breastplates of righteousness. This is not any ordinary piece of equipment; no, it guards our hearts. It is also not our own righteousness, for we put on the righteousness of Christ.

We must have our feet shod with the preparation of the gospel of peace and take peace to every place we stand as witnesses for Christ. The shield of faith is absolutely essential to cover your mind, emotions, and body. Like the Roman shield in Paul's day, it covers the entire torso. This is the area of our faith that Satan loves to fight. There will be fiery darts of sickness, trouble in your marriage, children acting up, and accusations against you. There could be a crisis such as a death in the family, a foreclosure, or a conflict in the church. Fiery darts will come! Shield up!

The helmet of salvation guards your mind. This protective weapon holds your thoughts together through prayer and meditation on the Word of God. Whatever the Enemy presents must first come to your mind, so don't speak negative words. Remember, death and life are in the power of the tongue (Proverbs 18:21). Speak life! Think on wholesome things. According to Philippians 4:8, God's peace protects our minds from being bombarded by negative thoughts and keeps them focused on God. He promises to keep us in perfect peace when our minds are fixed on Him (Isaiah 26:3).

Elect lady, where's your sword of the Spirit? This is the Word of God delivered from the mouth of a believer in a specific situation to confront the lies of the Enemy. So, be ready to release the precise word of God from your mouth.

Queen to Queen

If I were to name names, I would get into trouble, but I will say this: only four elect ladies have helped me by sharing and imparting their wisdom and knowledge. There is no judgment, shaming, blaming, or accusing in venting up. There is prayer, and, yes, sometimes tears. The one you vent to will advise you on the right thing to do. I say this to myself when I don't feel like doing the right thing: "It's not just for the people that I do the right thing but also because I don't want to let the name of the Lord down." In other words, turn it over to Jesus and you can smile for the rest of the day.

Venting down can expose your deepest fears and most intimate secrets. So, who's got you? Who knows who you are? Yes, we have our heavenly Father, but who is that tangible person who, when you slip up, doesn't condemn you? Can she be honest enough to tell you when you're wrong and support you when you fail?

I know an elect lady with a vibrant prayer life who goes before God and intervenes for the women and men of God. Yes, some of us are called to the assignment of intercessors. This is a God-given call. How do I see a call? I see a calling as a place or a position that you didn't necessarily put yourself in, but it comes as naturally to you as breathing. You can feel it pulling you toward it. A calling can be uncomfortable, but you press into it. We do it because of our love for God.

Have you ever faced a crazy situation at church where you wished you weren't the elect lady? You would normally tell the person who offended you exactly how you felt. But, as the elect lady, what stops you? What kicks in? For me, it's my love for God first. Secondly, it's not wanting to embarrass my husband—you notice I didn't say, my kids. There are things we hold back from telling our kids—but these children see, know, and hear. However, I focus on keeping my God-given integrity, even when I know what was done to hurt me. I remember who my God is, and I never forget heaven is watching.

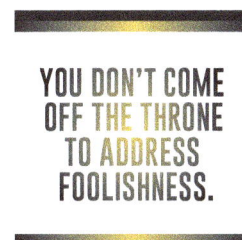
YOU DON'T COME OFF THE THRONE TO ADDRESS FOOLISHNESS.

Staying in a place without venting can be difficult. Oh, how I have wanted to vent and tell it like it is! But the voice of the Lord reminds me quietly in my ear who I am. "Lady Leisa, you are a queen. Queens don't come off the throne to address foolishness. You bow down low on your knees and watch Me work on your behalf."

I remember one time we expected the people to come and support our pastor, but only a faithful few came. I sat there as tears ran down my face, and I was wiping them just as fast. It was not by chance the message that night was from the first chapter of Habakkuk, as the prophet wailed to God, "How long will I cry for help, and You not hear?" The speaker that night let us know that God is in control, and He will take care of things in His timing. I had to learn to be patient and pray, not for God to punish anyone but for Him to keep my husband and pastor encouraged. I'm here to vent to God and tell Him what He already knows. Help us, God! We want to do this elect lady thing correctly.

Another Headspace

In a conversation with another elect lady, she said to me that God wants us to be in another headspace when dealing with some people. I didn't understand what she meant at the time and had to look up the word "headspace." "Headspace" in a firearm is the distance measured from the part of the caliber that stops forward motion. If the headspace is too short, ammunition that is in a specific place may not chamber or disarm properly. If the headspace is too large, the cartridge chase may rupture, possibly damaging the firearm and injuring the shooter. Basically, what she was saying was this: "Don't misfire with your words or deeds." The older saints used to say we need to keep the prayer wheel turning. Prayer is vital. In prayer, God will direct and instruct us on what we should or shouldn't do or say. So, keep a good spiritual headspace. We cannot afford to disgrace our Lord and Savior.

Ephesians 5:15 tells us to walk circumspectly, which means carefully. So, walk with caution, not as fools but as wise, redeeming the time because the days are evil. We are also to walk in the good works God has prepared in advance for us (Ephesians 2:10), in the truth (2 John 4), love (John 3:16), and wisdom in the way we interact with outsiders, making the most of every opportunity (Colossians 4:5-6). We are to follow peace with all men (Hebrews 12:14). Misfiring will cause you to walk as the foolish walk, though it seems right to them (Romans 1:21; Proverbs 12:15), whereas a wise person will seek God with all his heart. We don't want to walk out of fear and trepidation either. No, we want to walk with wisdom, so we won't fall into the traps the Enemy has laid for us, especially those that make us react before we think.

I've seen many wise, elect ladies who choose to pray and watch God change things. At the same time, some decide to fix it themselves without the help of God. Which elect lady is more than a conqueror? I've found out I can't do this without God. Don't get me wrong: I have been in a bad headspace many times. I misfired and had my share of apologies to make. So, you may be overlooked, misused, or mishandled, but God Himself will come to your aid. He will first rescue your wounded spirit, your thoughts, and your heart. He may minister to you in a dream, a song, or through His

Word. He'll let you know He's there for you to cast all your cares on Him because He cares for you. Jesus, your Advocate, will be there to plead your case.

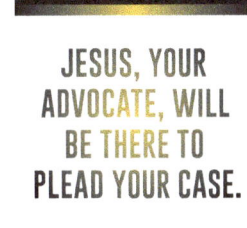

JESUS, YOUR ADVOCATE, WILL BE THERE TO PLEAD YOUR CASE.

I've even experienced God coming and filling my heart with so much love and compassion that I didn't need to tell anyone anything because I knew God was pleased with me. There was no need to run and tell anyone or get my point across. Social media is a place where I've seen many First Ladies vent. If I could get to them, I would tell them it's a dangerous place. No, stand firm because the ground you stand on is holy ground. It's a sure and proven foundation, walked down by many in the faith (see Hebrews Chapter 11).

Look Up and Live

Some have bent their knees in prayer to God for answers and help. There are also those with whom I have prayed for because they, need the strength of their sister. This is an example of the highest integrity and wisdom. Therefore, look up and live, First Lady! I know God has got this. He understands that at times you want to talk and vent, and He is there as your friend. You can trust Him and believe He has not forgotten you. We always ask whether we can depend on God, but I ask whether God can depend on us to be the elect ladies He's calling for, even in hard times.

When Ruth insisted on following her mother-in-law Naomi to Judah, she declared:

> Wherever you go, I will go; And wherever you lodge, I will lodge; Your people shall be my people, And your God, my God. (Ruth 1:16 NKJV)

There was no reason for her to follow Naomi because she, a Moabite, would not be welcomed in this foreign land and besides, her mother-in-law was destitute. But Ruth was fiercely loyal to her mother-in-law. Their circumstances were so similar: both had lost their husbands and both had to make a way for themselves; they needed each other to make that journey.

Little did they realize that favor and blessings were around the corner. As they took that road, the hand of God was already turning circumstances around for their good. Once they were in Bethlehem, as Ruth submitted to the elder woman, she found work gleaning in the grain fields. It was not by chance that Ruth happened to be gleaning in the field that belonged to their kinsman. Boaz was attracted to this young woman and showed her favor.

As the relationship between Ruth and Boaz began to develop, Naomi stepped up in her role as a mentor and instructed Ruth on how to approach this man for her covering, in other words, marriage. It was a bold step for a woman and a Moabite at that. Because Ruth followed the wise counsel of her mother-in-law, Ruth and Boaz were married and blessed with a son.

The wise counsel of a true woman of God, someone you can trust, can also help you achieve your heart's desires as you go through your God-given assignment. It is okay to go down on your knees in prayer and ask God who you can trust to mentor you.

For the Sake of the Cause

A First Lady once asked me what a pastor's wife should do when she doesn't want to go to church. The time will come when you may ask yourself whether you are helping or hindering the progress of the church because you disagree with the way things are being run. This will place you in a very precarious situation. Even at your worst, people are depending on you to conduct yourself according to the image they have of you in their minds. When you feel as though you don't want to go to church—and, yes, it is playing the role—you do it for the cause. It's not fake; it's sustaining the hope we see in the eyes of the people we serve.

While we are called to stretch ourselves, I am also huge on the elect lady taking a break when needed. There is something in my other profession called self-care. It is how we promote and maintain our mental and physical health and prevent disease. This is how you can reduce stress and contribute to your overall health care. I have learned to take care of myself because I'm the only me I have. Some say, "I don't have the funds to make a hobby out of it." But all the same, if I can save twenty here, fifty there, and get a group of women who I enjoy being around (who are not stressful and are drama-free) together and plan a trip to a spa, you can do the same. Go get a pedicure/manicure; enjoy being you! Get to know each other outside of the church.

I remember the times I was trying to be a helpful pastor's wife. My husband was going here and there, but he never asked me to accompany him. I felt isolated. One day, my sister, who had been a First Lady for

29 years, said to me, "Leisa, you need to get a life!" I cried and asked her what that meant. She said, "If you want to have longevity, you must find something you enjoy." And then she said, "Learn to enjoy your own company."

> **LEARN TO ENJOY YOUR OWN COMPANY.**

One of my favorite movies is *Pretty Woman*. When Julia Roberts' character, Vivian Ward, decides she wants to live a clean life, she goes and gives her friend some money and tells her plans to her. Kit De Luca replies, "Take care of you." I repeat that to every elect lady who wants to give up and throw in the towel: "Take care of yourself; love yourself; be there for yourself… and be kind to yourself." Oliver Goldsmith once said, "Live to fight another day." We often forget we are human and can only bear so much. Take full advantage of the rest Jesus gives your mind, body, and soul.

> Come to me all of you who are tired from carrying heavy loads, and I will give you rest. (Matthew 11:28 GNTD)

Value Yourself

Learn to value yourself. The definition of "value" is something considered important. So, count as valuable those who value you. This is not the cliché, "Do to others as they do unto you." That's not what I'm saying. What I'm saying is that if you have relationships with people who value your time, company, smile, acquisition, and you as a person, then you should value them the same way. Never let anyone make you feel small or inadequate. I've heard people say, "It doesn't matter what other people think." Well, it does matter if you give it power. Eleanor Roosevelt once said, "Remember always that you not only have the right to be an individual, but you have an obligation to want to be. You cannot make any useful contribution in life unless you do this."

So be the valued, wonderful, beautiful, intelligent, smart, goal-filled woman of God you were meant to be. Your value is not in your looks; your value is in the intentions and motives of your heart. I know it's hard sometimes. I've found that I've had to be my biggest cheerleader in those times when I felt my value was less than palatable. I had to ask myself why I do what I do, and it always comes back to doing what I do, serving how I serve, because of my love for God and His people. This is something that always gives me value. I don't serve with any hidden agenda. The same goes for leading the men, women, and children counting on us for guidance. They must feel they are worthwhile and know that you are here to do what God wants you to do: help direct His people to Him to find their way out of situations.

Submitting our ways and desires to God is what makes us valuable. We are the righteousness of God. We are His children and His prized possessions. You're valuable to God; now be valuable to yourself. Enjoy life; have fun; do something you've never done before. If you value yourself, people will value you. If you don't value yourself, you'll see that others won't value you either. I once heard a bishop ask, "Where does a leader go to share his heart without fear, or a foul being called on them?" We don't know. That's why we say a prayer and ask God what to do:

> Even though the actions of godly and wise people are in God's hands, no one knows whether God will show them favor. (Ecclesiastes 9:1 NLT)

No man knows whether people will respond to him in love or hate; anything awaits him. No matter how you feel or who you may choose to vent to, at the end of the day, ask God.

PRAYER

Dear God, please give us the strength to conquer every obstacle in our path. We believe the Word is our source of strength in all things. Thank You for being our guiding light and shelter in the storm. We believe You will cause favor to be our portion. At times when we feel weak and tired, You will be the wind at our back. We lift You high, Lord, above our problems. You are our peace and calm. In Jesus' name, Amen.

WRITE YOUR AFFIRMATION OF EMPOWERMENT

_____
_____
_____
_____
_____
_____
_____
_____
_____
_____

CHAPTER 4

GRACE

And now I commend you to God and to the word of his grace, which is able to build you up and to give you the inheritance among all those who are sanctified. (Acts 20:32 ESV)

I have seen our church go through so many changes, from membership growth to membership decline. In those times of decline, I knew my family's sacrifice was inevitable. There were times when our personal finances were given to help the church's needs. I've seen my husband, my pastor, go without for the sake of the cause. I knew the truth. I knew his heart for the church's finances. Even though the church members blessed us, if there was a need, he would do his best to meet it. There were times I would ask myself if *we* were the sacrifice.

So, what is grace but simple elegance or refinement of movement? I learned to go with the flow and God never let us down. We always made it through the journey though it was not always easy walking in grace. You must develop a relationship with God. Grace allows you to see your situation in a way that assures you of God's promises.

You see, before you become gold, you must be tested. Grace shows you what you are made of, whether you are 10k, 14k, 18k, 22k, or 24k gold. When gold is tested, it goes through the refiner's fire to be purified. Then it receives the official mark of its authenticity. Gold goes through a stress test, so even through stress, we maintain our gracefulness. An elect lady once told me, "I have finally figured it out: I'm his wife, his helpmate, his lover, his friend, the pastor's wife, and his sounding board."

If God has deemed you worthy, there must be an official mark:

> Nevertheless the foundation of God standeth sure, having this seal, The Lord knoweth them that are his. And, let everyone that nameth the name of Christ depart from iniquity. (2 Timothy 2:19)

> And they shall be mine, saith the LORD of hosts, in that day when I make up my jewels. (Malachi 3:17)

Elect ladies, we are jewels. We walk beside God's chosen vessels. We are graced to encourage and pray for them.

But I am also the people's spiritual mother. According to the Myers-Briggs Type Indicator, I have an INFPS personality often described as an "idealist" or "mediator." The INFPS is an abbreviation for sixteen different personality types: the duty fulfiller, the mechanic, the nurturer, the artist, the protector, the idealist, the scientist, the thinker, the doer, the guardian, the performer, the caregiver, the inspirer, the giver, the visionary, and the executive. With all these personalities combined in my make-up, it takes God to help me pass the stress test gracefully.

> Let this mind be in you, which was also in Christ Jesus.
> (Philippians 2:5 NKJV)

This speaks of our attitude to Jesus. He always wanted to please His Father. Gold goes through a magnet test: if it pulls forward or sticks, it is fake. In the same way, grace allows us to be real. We must be careful not to be fake. Be true to yourself. Don't get lost in the position depending on your denomination, or the grace will fade away. Elect lady, get a life beyond the church. Do something you enjoy.

My father and mother pastored together for thirty years. When my father died because my mother always had a life filled with doing things she enjoyed, she was able to stay strong. She was always full of grace, and like pure gold, she didn't let the position stick to her. She embraced her calling and she knew there was also ministry in her. She worked out and is yet working out her own salvation with fear and trembling. Gold goes through the acid test to see how it will react. As a pastor's wife, there will be times when you will get burned by misunderstandings, lies, and deceit, to see if you will react too.

Keep Sweet

Pastor Slaughter Sr. would say: "Keep sweet, keep smiling, and keep stepping." You keep sweet to honor God; you keep smiling so they don't know they're getting to you, and you keep stepping because it doesn't matter. Through grace, we walk out our lives in public because somebody is always watching.

Mums the word if you, like me, watched other pastors' wives, operate in the capacity of a First Lady; but you yourself never knew how to walk in this calling until you had to put the First Lady pumps on your own feet? Walk in your season. It's your time for grace. An elect lady said to me, "I don't sing, and I'm not good at public speaking. But I'm my pastor/husband's biggest supporter, his cheerleader, his sounding board, and his confidante. I am his soft place to land. Gracefully, I am 'The Pastor's Wife!'" What a testimony!

What is grace unless you maintain your composure under pressure? It's inherent in your calling as God told the prophet Jeremiah:

> I knew you before you were formed within your mother's womb; before you were born, I sanctified you and appointed you as my spokesman to the world.
>
> (Jeremiah 1:5 TLB)

He knew you and this is what He had destined for you. Listen to His words to you: "I knew you before I formed you in your mother's womb. Before you were born, I set you apart and anointed you as my prophet to the nations. You were handpicked. You were chosen for this ministry through grace."

Pastors' wives are a rare breed, gifts. We are the fragrance of the house. My pastor is the sandalwood stick, and we carry the sweet savor of the Holy Ghost everywhere we go. Embrace the calling with the grace God has given you. Out of all the women in the world, He has chosen you. With all your imperfections and flaws, He has chosen you to walk beside His heartbeat, the man of God. You are the pastor's wife.

You are a wise and courageous woman like Abigail in 1 Samuel Chapter 2. Her husband, Nabal, was a fool according to the Bible because he denied David and his men provision in an emergency. But Abigail was wise. She knew she was married to a foolish man but through her courage and initiative, she saved her whole family from the wrath of David, the soon-to-be king. When Nabal died, David took Abigail as his second wife. The Bible describes her as beautiful and intelligent.

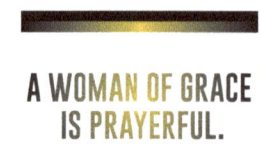

At times, you will also have to be wise— not to say your man of God is foolish. But understand the things of God; have an open ear; be watchful in prayer; know the Word of God; cover your family for God's divine protection, and you, too, will be wise. God will use you to pray for healing and deliverance over your entire church family. A woman of grace is prayerful.

One day while in our early morning prayer—4:00 a.m. to be exact, I read this scripture:

> But those who fail to find me harm themselves; all who hate me love death. (Proverbs 8:36 NIV)

At the time, five of my sisters and my mother were all pastor's wives. This entire chapter is talking about wisdom personified as a woman instructing us on how we are to pursue her. When I asked God for His wisdom, knowledge, and understanding, He told me to watch my motives. Motives stem from the heart, which means, watching your reason for doing anything and letting it be pure. I have not always hit the mark. There were times I said what I wanted to say and did what I wanted to do. This did not please God, for our goal is to please Him in grace. When we move in grace, our positions are admirable.

Too Big for You

A close elect lady friend of mine had physical health challenges. She and I were so very different. She was a little quieter in her spirit, and you would never know by her face if anything had gotten under her skin. She told me a story of a woman in her church who shared a dream she had about her. The woman came to her crying and telling her that in her dream, my friend wasn't with them anymore. She said to my friend, "I was standing in your place in front of the church in your clothes, but your clothes were too big for me. What do you think that means?"

My elect lady friend told me, "I couldn't believe what I was hearing! This young girl thought I was either sick or dying!" The answer my friend gave this young woman was priceless! She said she looked the young woman squarely in her eyes and said to her, "What your dream means is the position you think you want is too big for you." Touché! A woman of grace makes this position look easy. God guides and upholds us as we do the will of the One who has graced us with the ability.

An Ear of Corn

If you know my personality, then you know that I'm very outspoken and tell it like it is. This calling has taught me it's not always necessary to speak your mind. So, one day, I went to my mother crying and feeling bad because something had happened, and I could not defend myself. I felt like a weak-kneed person because I had to surrender my will to the will of God. My mother said something to me I will never forget. She said, "You are like an ear of corn with the shuck still on it; you have layers God is trying to get rid of." There were things I didn't necessarily want to change because I felt I needed my extra—you know—my extra mouth, extra attitude. They helped me to be who I was. I'd forgotten this Scripture:

If any man is in Christ, he is a new creature. (2 Corinthians 5:17 NKJV)

YOU HAVE LAYERS GOD IS TRYING TO GET RID OF.

Through grace, God has taken layers of shuck off me. The more you are exposed, the more anointed and prayed up you become. When you have been gracefully shucked, what should have killed you will roll off like water on a duck's back.

In ministry, we think that because we are saved, offenses will not affect us. On the contrary, I remember a time when grace had to be extended as we watched marriages break up and families go through tough times. I remember this pastor and his wife who were breaking up. I was upset with the husband because I felt it was his fault. Then an unsaved man who knew them as well said to me, "Why are you doing more than God? Doesn't God love him too?"

I stood back and replied, "Yes, He does." Grace is not something God extends exclusively to us; it's something we should extend to others.

Chess Pieces

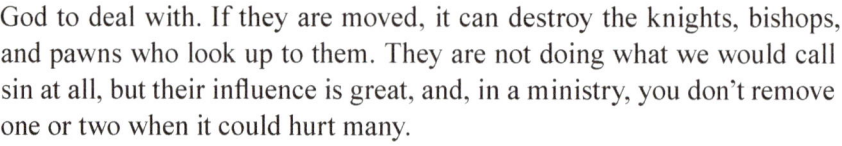

Now, when we look at people in our churches, some are like chess pieces. The two most important pieces on the board are the king and queen; after those, it's the rooks. Well, we have rooks on the board who we must leave to God to deal with. If they are moved, it can destroy the knights, bishops, and pawns who look up to them. They are not doing what we would call sin at all, but their influence is great, and, in a ministry, you don't remove one or two when it could hurt many.

The Bible says to let the wheat and the tares grow together and, in due time, God will separate them:

> Let both grow together until the harvest: and in the time of harvest, I will say to the reapers, Gather ye together first the tares, and bind them in bundles to burn them: but gather the wheat into my barn. (Matthew 13:30)

Get some rest; don't take things so personally. I say if these people are not afraid of God, who are you?

On the other hand, some older women have so much grace and poise about themselves. They could teach us a lot. I appreciate them most of all because they taught me how to pray. They were never defensive. I watched when my mother was disrespected, and she never lost her calm. She would often say, "If I get out of character that will help them, but if I stay graceful it will always help me." In fact, I've noticed that other people come to the defense of the most graceful elect ladies. They help them and take care of the disrespectful ones. This happens, especially if you are truly honest, and people respect you.

Some say they're not the kind of First Ladies who will let anyone disrespect them. You don't have to fight for yourself, but you do need to always keep yourself in check. Sometimes, it's not going to matter; you're not going to please everyone all the time. But you want to please God, the ultimate Judge. So, stay graceful; stay approachable, and be kind. Most of all, make sure it's authentic. People can tell when you are pretending. It will eventually come out, so be the best version of yourself that you can be. If you put God first, you won't make the mistake of coming up short. God will cover you. Grace looks good on you!

The Greatest Servant

Jesus was our example of the greatest servant. He washed the disciples' feet. He fed the hungry and poor. He healed the sick and lame. He served with purpose.

> The greatest among you will be your servant.
> (Matthew 23:11 NIV)

The greatest elect lady is not called to just wear a hat and look pretty; she's the pretty lady who works in her ministry. I have gone to several churches where they have established that the First Lady should not work as hard as First Ladies or elect ladies do in other churches. That's their choice.

Ministry is almost like a relationship. It is a covenant and, yes, it is work! Not all work is hard; much of it is pleasant and fulfilling. I love to see the fruit of my labor. I love to get involved in whatever is going on in the ministry. When our church goes out to witness, I want to be there. If they are going to the church to clean, I want to be there too! Not out of obligation, but because of my love for ministry in every aspect, and it's just my makeup. Now, don't get me wrong; if this is not what you do, and God has given you the grace to be the helpmate suitable for your husband/pastor, then do your part. We're all alike because we have been given the great charge of looking after and complementing the man of God.

In our respective roles, we have a God-given obligation that we mustn't forget:

> My dear brothers and sisters, take note of this: Everyone should be quick to listen, slow to speak and slow to become angry. (James 1:19 NIV)

In my years of being an elect lady, I have realized you can't win them all. You can't please them all, but you can love them all with the love of Christ. At times, I knew I was the target, but let's just say most of the time, I passed the test. However, when I failed to hear the voice of God, I would spend the night talking to Him, and asking Him to forgive me for ignoring His gentle, still, small voice that was encouraging me to stay focused. Grace expressed gently in the face of conflicts does not make us weak. Rather, it allows God to lead us to the next assignment. Isn't it our goal to please God with our actions? Grace helps us to activate this.

The Word of God instructs us in Isaiah 51:6, to wear this world like a loose garment. That doesn't mean we don't care about the ministry or what comes with it. No, we become the heroines of our own stories; we love on ourselves, see to our own needs, and care about ourselves without guilt. Wear this world and its burdens like a kimono, open in the front, easy on and easy off. Take off everything that keeps you from being the best you. Live in grace, walk in promise, and rest in the Lord.

Grace

PRAYER

Lord Jesus, help me to walk in grace. Help me to embrace the challenges You allow in my life, and to disregard those challenges not meant for my life. Give me the ability to know the difference. In Jesus' name. Amen.

WRITE YOUR AFFIRMATION OF GRATITUDE

_____

_____

_____

_____

_____

_____

_____

_____

_____

CHAPTER 5

MY HUBBY, MY LOVER, MY FRIEND

> And I will give you pastors according to mine heart, which shall feed you with knowledge and understanding. (Jeremiah 3:15)

Let's explore the blessing of being called to walk alongside the man God says is after His own heart. Jeremiah declares:

> I knew you before I formed you in your mother's womb, before you were born I set you apart and anointed you as my prophet to the nations. (Jeremiah 1:5 NIV)

Being a First Lady is a position I can say most of us didn't ask for. But know this: you were hand-selected for this ministry, and this is the place God has given to you.

Whatever role you play as an elect lady, be the best you can be. Some are public speakers. Some are caregivers just to their husbands/pastors and children. Some are involved in ministry. Some work outside of the home. Some of us are on the church administrative team. Remember, people are watching and can see if you and your husband are friends or if you're playing a role. A man once told my husband that when my husband/pastor asked the church to stand, and I stood that he was glad I did. He said, "We watch to see your obedience, and we watch you when he preaches."

> Ye are our epistle written in our hearts, known and read of all men. (2 Corinthians 3:2)

Where's My Wife?

Above all, never forget your husband is a man, and he needs you as a woman to be beside him. As a pastor's daughter (aka PK), I knew how to work in the church. My father taught my sisters and me how to work in every area of ministry. I could open and close the doors of the church, lift an offering, sing, play a little, speak, and teach whatever and wherever needed. I tried to fulfill all these roles as an elect lady and would come home exhausted. My husband/pastor would ask me "Where's my wife—not the elect lady—but my wife?" I thought I was doing all this church work to help him, but he said to me, "When I married you, you were not an elect lady. You gave *me* attention. Now you're tired trying to keep up with church obligations."

My hubby, my friend, needed that woman he married. I had no clue she was missed. I thought I was pleasing him by working at the church. But he wanted his wife. The church can take so much of your time as it did at the beginning of our ministry, but you must make time for each other.

> Marriage should be honored by all, and the marriage bed kept pure. (Hebrews 13:4a)

In our sexual relationship, the bed is kept pure; it is shared only with husband and wife. When we enter into marriage with our husbands, the only thing I can say is to repeat what Bishop T.D. Jakes said, "I stop where the Bible stops." Your desires and the things you do with your spouse is your business. However, we must maintain a healthy relationship in our marriage. There are reasons why we may not be intimate for a season; sickness is one. Fasting is another. In our wedding vows, we promised we'd be there for one another: in sickness and in health.

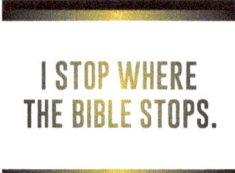

I STOP WHERE THE BIBLE STOPS.

I have had the privilege of spending time with a lot of women whose pastors/husbands are now deceased. The one thing they don't regret is having a loving, caring, intimate relationship with their husbands. One of you might be more sexual than the other. Like I said, my husband used to say to me don't give it out to the church and then when you get home, you have none left for me. Oops! now you know who is more sexual than the other in my house lol. So, I asked God to help me. I was blessed to be instructed by older women. One, in particular, was Mother Wade. She would help us out by saying if your husband is from the streets his knowledge may be different than someone that never left the church. She would tell us to pray and ask God to make us compatible.

First Lady you got this. I know this area can be challenging. But be the women he married. Keep the element of surprise. Remember that what works for you all works for you. "It's your thang."

It Ain't About Leah

I have been in a lot of women's gathering where I have seen First Ladies worried about the women in their churches. Women may speak to the pastor then walk by the First Lady without saying a word. Hear me and hear me good: I have a husband who works a secular job. I know he sees beautiful women all day, every day. I keep myself up. I put that Ruby Woo red lipstick on when I go to his job looking cute. Laugh out loud.

In Genesis, Jacob wanted Rachel. But through some trickery, his father-in-law gave him Leah her older sister instead. The Bible says Leah had weak eyes. Listen, Rachel was getting jealous of her sister when Leah was bearing children and Rachel could not get pregnant. But Jacob did not love Leah. Rachel forgot that she had his heart.

> GIRL, I KNOW WHO HE GOES HOME WITH.

I'm only equipped to talk about the men of God who have integrity, who truly love God, and genuinely love their wife. I've seen women make a concerted effort to speak to my husband and not even smile at me. Girl, I know who he goes home with. I know who carries his heart and mind. It ain't about Leah; it's about the covenant we made before God. First Lady, fight the jealous spirit. Rebuke it! The Bible says it's as cruel as the grave.

We are wise women who build our homes. Failure is not an option. My husband and I made a promise to each other over 26 years ago: "If it makes you uncomfortable and you tell me, I won't do it." It's all about us. Now, I have to admit that some pastors love the attention even at the expense of the First Lady. If that's your husband, I say turn it over to Jesus. I promise you, if he is a true man of God, things will change.

Let me make this clear there have been cases where the First Lady did all she could do and it didn't matter how she cooked, cleaned, worked, or looked pretty. I will not put my mouth on this Pastor. I will say this: First Lady you are not alone. Writing this book has given me a deeper respect for you in this regard. You know there are souls attached to his unscrupulous behavior. Your loneliness and your tears have not gone unnoticed. When you cry, God takes notice. I thank the Lord for responding with concern and care. A Pastor's wife once said to me, "There is a look my husband gives when he wants me. I saw him give that look to someone else." At the end of the day, we must pray and ask God what direction to take. We cannot make anyone do right; it's a heart thing.

> It is not what goes into the mouth of a man that defiles and dishonors him, but what comes out of the mouth, this defiles and dishonors him. (Matthew 15:11 AMP)

Just like there are superheroes, there are villains. Just like there's a good shepherd, there are hirelings. The good shepherd cares for his sheep. He feeds them the right kind of food. A good shepherd will die for his sheep in order to keep them out of harm's way. The good shepherd follows after the example Jesus gave in the gospel of John:

> Again Jesus said, "Simon son of John, do you love me?" He answered, "Yes, Lord, you know that I love you." Jesus said, "Take care of my sheep." (John 21:16 NIV)

However, the hireling doesn't care for the sheep:

> The hired hand is not the shepherd and does not own the sheep. So when he sees the wolf coming, he abandons the sheep and runs away. Then the wolf attacks the flock and scatters it. The man runs away because he is a hired hand and cares nothing for the sheep. (John 10:12-13 NIV)

First Lady, I'm in prayer continually for you. I ask God to protect your heart and your mind. I have asked some why they stay with wayward husbands. They tell me they stay for their love of the people of God and cover their husbands in prayer, hoping their man of God will seek help or until God says differently. I have seen it play out both ways. I remember it's God's decision to make.

Until then, in the words of Bishop Hezekiah Walker:

I pray for you.

You pray for me.

I love you.

I need you to survive.

I won't harm you with words from my mouth.

I love you.

I need you to survive.

You are important to me.

I need you to survive.

First Lady, you are forever in my heart.

The Approach Is Key

Be his friend and his friendly critic.
This is the part of being an elect lady I used
to neglect the most. But through prayer, God has given me a watchful eye, so I can discern when something is not right without being judgmental. I go with a quiet spirit and the Word of God.

Many times, in the past, I've tried to get my pastor/husband to listen to me about a matter. My approach needed to be respectful. I had to be mindful that, even though he's my husband, he's also God's man for the set time. One day, an elect lady friend of mine told me to stop talking and pray. She told me if I am watchful in prayer and if my husband is a true man of God, he will either ask you what you think about a situation, or he will find out for himself through praying for God's direction. Let me make this clear; there have been times I messed up and even said the dreaded words, "I told you so!" Thank God my husband didn't hold that against me!

AGREE TO DISAGREE WITHOUT BEING DISAGREEABLE.

Feeling like you are being heard is important. We have had to agree to disagree without being disagreeable. I didn't always understand him and there were times when what I said got lost in translation. However, that's when the Word of God would come into play, "In all thy getting, get understanding" (Proverbs 4:7). That was a mutual goal.

Above all, we are friends. When I explore the word "friend," the definition that comes to mind is "a person who is loyal, with integrity, trustworthy, honest, and a secret keeper." To me, this is what a friend looks like. I have told my friends in the past, "You are my friends because we speak the truth to one another." So, my husband and I value frankness and openness with each other.

There is one experience I will never forget. I remember watching my husband take care of the needs of the church despite our financial situation. We weren't in ministry that long, and our various tasks and obligations were intertwined. Well, I tell you there will always be someone who wants to see you fail. I mean, the church is a pretty big size, a two-story building about ten thousand square feet. When we became servants of the house, and times got hard, people chose sides, and some even left during that time. Nevertheless, my husband made sure the house of God was taken care of. I cannot say that I was always supportive, but I will say I was watching. I saw he wanted to survive. He wanted that church to thrive, and he wanted the people to see he loved them and the ministry.

What the people didn't know was that we were getting notices from the bank telling us that they were going to foreclose on our house. They were going to take the house we had worked so hard to get. My husband would always assure me that things were going to work out and it was going to be okay. I never saw him sweat or become stressed out. I was stressing out enough for the both of us. He didn't want me to see how he felt. My husband, my friend, would still go to church and preach as if nothing was out of the ordinary.

Well, on this one particular Monday, we got another notice. This time I guess I'd had just about enough. I started packing the house and taking pictures down. I didn't believe anything better was going to happen for us, but I didn't want to be blindsided. I was going to pack up all my memories and get out of that house!

That evening, my husband and I attended a church conference. It was the "Restoration Conference." The prophet who was speaking that night called me out. He told me to go home and take everything out of the boxes because God was going to work a miracle. You don't know me. I said okay, but, needless to say, I didn't do it, although my husband, my pastor, and my friend, encouraged me to take the things out of the boxes.

The fourth Sunday in May came around. My husband was preaching the unadulterated Word of God with great gusto as he always did. He moved his hands in circles and said these words, "God is getting ready to change somebody's paperwork—someone's paperwork is getting mixed up!"

I said, "Lord, I hope it's us!"

We have something in our denomination called a "Convocation." This is when churches from all over the region come together for one week and worship together in the same place. I was my Bishop's wife's attendant— or should I say—armor bearer. That means from the beginning to the end of the meeting I was there by her side to make sure she and her guests had what they needed. I love this position.

On the last day of the convocation, which was on a Sunday, Prophet Todd Hall was the speaker for that day. He asked for a specific dollar amount for people to give as an offering. My husband gave what he asked for and the prophet told my husband that, "things were going to change, by this time tomorrow." When my husband wrote the check, I was thinking to myself we still needed to pay to get out of the parking garage. Can you believe it? We had no money to pay the attendant to get our car out of the parking garage. Thankfully, a pastor from within our Reformation came and paid for us to get our car out of the parking garage. You talk about embarrassing! We drove all the way home in silence. I had nothing to say. I just knew we needed to continue preparing to move out of our home.

Have you ever sealed your own fate? I forgot that God is our provider. I forgot He is a way maker. When we got home, I saw a large envelope. It was from our mortgage company. I opened the envelope, and there was a contract offering us a modification cutting our mortgage payments by more than half, and giving us an extension to 30 years. I didn't know if I was really reading the letter right or understanding the contract. I called out to my husband, "You need to read this!"

He just replied, "I can't take any bad news," he said. "I can't do anything about it tonight anyway. I'll wait until Monday."

"No, I think you need to read this because I don't know if I'm understanding what I'm reading."

He took the contract and looked over it and then I looked over it again. We were both still unsure about what we were reading so we called a bishop friend of ours who also happened to be a broker. We read the contract to him, and he yelled to my husband, "Sign it now! Take it to the post office first thing in the morning and overnight it." He said, "I've never seen an offer like that before!"

Remember that was on a Sunday night so needless to say, first thing Monday morning, I was at the post office, return receipt requested and certified. Three days later, I got a call from the mortgage company saying, "We don't know what happened; your paperwork got mixed up—but we hope that in good faith, you'll let us send you the offer we were going to send." I asked if the contract we received was valid, and they said yes it was. So, we took the offer, and there was nothing the mortgage company could do.

My Salute

I included this testimony in this book because I've seen my husband, my pastor, and my friend, pray through hard times. I've seen him get us through weary nights, handling business like no other, and take on the responsibility of supporting a wife and eight children—plus a church family, and never once complain. Yes, there've been hard days. But when he wanted to give up (but he didn't tell me), he would just say, "I believe God!" I salute him in this book. He truly cares about the people of God and is genuinely concerned about their struggles.

Our children never knew how hard we really had it. They knew there were times when things were a little tough, but God still blessed us to be able to enjoy family outings and go to most of the places we wanted to go. I know that it was all because of my husband, my friend, and my pastor's faithfulness to God.

I encourage you today, First Ladies, elect ladies, and pastors' wives, do your best to help keep your husband/pastor strong. Some mornings I get up at 5 a.m. and pray for him. I let him hear me as I lay my hands on him because I realize I survived because he survived. So, I pray for God's strength over the man that is after God's own heart.

God not only chose the man of God who is after His heart, but He also chose you because you have brought favor to his life. The Bible says we are our husbands' favor. The Father chose you to love on the man, the pastor, the husband, so don't complain; be his biggest cheerleader—sometimes his greatest critic. But most times, be his lover, his peace, and a soft place for him to lay his head. I often tell my husband how grateful I am to know the one thing that no one else in any church, jurisdiction, or district can have is our love. It's ours. So, we nourish it, covet more of it, and do whatever it takes to keep it alive. It's the one thing, elect lady, the church can't take or touch. It's what God has given us—to love and care for each other "until death do us part."

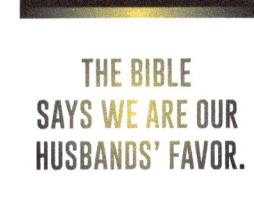

THE BIBLE SAYS WE ARE OUR HUSBANDS' FAVOR.

If I were to say it has always been easy, I would not be telling the truth. There was a time when we struggled, not because we weren't close partners or we didn't believe in God, but because others didn't believe in Him. My friend, as the First Lady, it is not always easy to understand what decisions or positions to take, but I still reside in my home comfortably and securely with my husband and two of our eight children. God has been faithful.

When walking alongside the man of God, you will see his growth. Though challenges will come your way, continue to hold the man of God up in prayer. He will be misunderstood at times and praised at other times.

First Ladies, Can We Talk?

We salute every man of God walking in his calling. It is a great task. When I think about a pastor, I don't think about it the way I used to with my father. I see the blood, sweat, tears, time, and energy. If the average pastor was paid for everything he does for the body of Christ, he would be a millionaire.

Pray for the Shepherd

Your pastor is your shepherd. There is a difference between a shepherd and a hireling. As Jesus told us, the primary difference is their motivation for attending to the sheep. The hireling does it for his own benefit; the shepherd does it for the benefit of the sheep. The shepherd stands beside you when things get tough and does what he can to protect and care for his sheep. People, I married a true shepherd of God. He is a man who is proud of me and who I am proud of. He is my pastor, husband, and friend.

First Ladies, can we talk? If your pastor/husband is a man of integrity, stay smiling; stay prayerful, and always be watchful because your adversary, the Devil comes as a roaring lion seeking whom he may devour (1 Peter 5:8). Our job is to make sure our families and our husbands are not easy prey. We must watch by staying on our knees and abiding in the Word of God. As a shepherd, sometimes your hubby, your friend, won't share secrets with you. Nevertheless, lift him up. Ask God to lead and guide you into all truth, lacking nothing, and strengthening his mind, body, and spirit. It is your responsibility to pray for your man of God. My prayer for my husband/pastor goes something like this:

"I thank You, God, for the man You've given me. Strengthen him daily. Keep him safe from all hurt, harm, and danger. Put a shield of protection around his body and keep him from the plans of the Enemy. Watch him as he goes about Your business. Let no sickness or disease come by his dwelling, keep him sound in mind and body, and bring Your Word to him in season. As he ministers Your Word to Your people, feed the sheep You have entrusted to Him. As he does these things, cover us in Your blood with all strength, power, and might. Help him to be the father he needs to be. Help him to be the husband he needs to be for me. Help me to be the wife he needs me to be. Let us work together in unity with nothing lacking and nothing missing. Help us to get along. Help us to understand one another. Help us to love one another. Help us to endeavor to keep the unity of the spirit in the bond of peace. In Jesus' name, I pray. Amen."

First Lady, can we talk? Pray for your husband even when he doesn't know you're praying. Lay hands on him and anoint him with oil. Watch God take both of you where you need to go in Him. Some of our greatest adversities and embarrassments have brought my husband and me to a deeper understanding of one another—perfect? Absolutely not—but willing to pursue peace and happiness? Absolutely.

As one who was brought up as a PK, I saw things that I said I would never ever want to go through or allow. Now, there I was, watching how my husband made sure the church was being taken care of, and sometimes with our household funds.

The Suburban

I can recall going through one of the most embarrassing moments ever in our lives. I was inside of the church when one of the young children came running to tell me, "Lady Johnson, there's a man outside taking your truck!" As I walked to the door, I saw a tow truck getting ready to tow our Suburban. I asked the man if he would let me drive my truck around the corner to get our things out of it, and he allowed me to do that.

We still had to go into the church for our worship service. So, we gathered our composure and went into the sanctuary as if nothing had happened. I could see the anguish on my husband's face, and I'm sure he saw the same on mine. We finished the service and now had to get a ride home. It didn't matter that we knew we would be getting our car back on Monday; what mattered was how my husband handled everything. I never saw him sweat, and I never heard him complain. What I saw was the man who became a fixer of all problems for me and our children. I saw my hubby and my friend, and I think that was the day I began trusting him even more.

The responsibility that's on our husbands is great. They must obey God while leading those who want to be shepherded, as well as see to the welfare of their families. To be honest with you, the only thing that comes before me, the elect lady, is God. I don't know about you, but I like my unique position. I'm his wide receiver: whatever vision he casts I catch it and run with it to help it come to fruition.

PRAYER

Father, I thank You for allowing us to have the awesome privilege of being examples of love, kindness, joy, and strength. It is an honor to display the fruit of the Spirit. We desire to be bold in making a difference for Your glory. We honor You and we are willing to show the world Your awesomeness by the way we live. Lord, even when under pressure, we are strong through prayer. We focus on Your Word, which will enable us to stand in times of heaviness. O Lord, we thank You for being so faithful. We are the helpmates to the man of God. As we serve him, we serve You with our whole hearts. Stabilize our emotions as we look to the cross. We declare that we are blessed with a godly union. In Jesus' name. Amen.

WRITE YOUR AFFIRMATION OF A COVENANT RELATIONSHIP

_____

_____

_____

_____

_____

_____

_____

_____

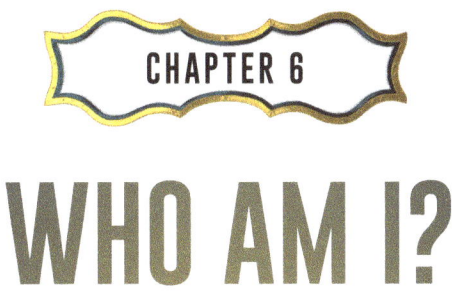

CHAPTER 6

WHO AM I?

For this is a gracious thing, when, mindful of God, one endures sorrows while suffering unjustly. (1 Peter 2:19 ESV)

She loved being his wife and the mother of his children but was still trying to embrace the pastor side of the relationship. She was frustrated. Her husband had received an elevation that was wonderful, but her concern was more of his time would be spent away from their family. So, she asked a few good questions: "Where do I fit in? Where's the balance? Do I get a husband at home and not a pastor, or should I expect to always deal with a pastor/husband?"

If you are honest, you have felt the same. I told my husband that the church is first to him, only for him to say, "I'm not married to the church. I'm married to Leisa." But that was not how it seemed at times. The fact is I had to learn to switch between my husband and my pastor, and still take care of myself.

In 2005, the new Disney movie *Cinderella* was playing in the theaters. Cinderella was given this nickname by her evil stepsisters because of the ash on her face from all the dusting and cleaning she was made to do. However, she embraced the name; she worked hard; she was kind, and she had courage. This made me think about Isaiah 61:3 that says, "I will give you beauty for ashes". Had her stepmother and her stepsisters known that they were talking to greatness, they probably would have treated her better, because there was a queen inside of her, a royal priesthood, a holy nation.

My point is this, my sister: the queen of purpose cannot be diminished by a thought or an action. She was already the elect. She was already called out. She was already chosen to be everything she would need to be.

You see, the queen was already inside of her. It's already inside of you too! God knew what He was doing when He selected you; when He called your pastor/husband, He had you in mind too.

Why Me?

The year 2005 was an uncertain year for me. A year into the calling, my friends began to change—some by choice—and several friendships were destroyed. Trying to wrap your mind around being who you're called to be and what some people would expect of you, you ask yourself, "Do I wear hats and a church suit? Do I speak or be quiet?"

Cinderella was kind, even though they were mean to her. One thing I've learned is if you truly trust God, He will give you beauty for your ashes as He promised in Isaiah. There were times I cried. I wanted to know why I had to be the one chosen for this daunting task, for this misunderstood life, for this life under a microscope—me and my children.

Then God spoke to me through Isaiah 43:19:

> Behold, I will do a new thing, now it shall spring forth;
> Shall you not know it? I will even make a road in the
> wilderness and rivers in the desert. (NKJV)

At times, I felt as though I was in a dry, lonely place, not knowing that this was the solitude I needed to mold me into who God said I am. I didn't see it then, but through the thirst and the hunger that came with every trial and tribulation, I got to know more about who God was. This was necessary as the apostle Paul declares:

> Yet indeed I also count all things loss for the excellence of
> the knowledge of Christ Jesus my Lord, for whom I have
> suffered the loss of all things, and count them as rubbish, that
> I may gain Christ … that I may know Him and the power of
> His resurrection, and the fellowship of His sufferings, being
> conformed to His death. (Philippians 3:8, 10 NKJV)

The Fellowship of Suffering

In Greek, the word "conformable" means to be complete," "obedient," and "ready to follow." Like Paul, I wanted to know my God, so I was ready to be content and obedient to His will. I wanted to get to know Him in the fellowship of suffering and the power of His resurrection. I wanted to please God more than I wanted to please myself. He did it for me from the time I was a young girl of eighteen when I told God, yes, for the hundredth time. Then he did it again at twenty-two when I told Him yes again—and I've never looked back. I had no idea the journey my life would take.

I once visited a Biblical Garden in Grass Valley, California, where there is a labyrinth. It looked like a maze, but I found out it was a little different." A maze is a complex branching multicausal, which involves choices, while a labyrinth is a unicursal". It only has one single non-branching path that leads you to the center. Think of all our separate paths and journeys we will take, and after we get through going in circles and through mazes, we find out who we are, even then God still desires to be the center of our lives.

As pastors' wives, it's easy to second-guess ourselves and wonder if we're doing any good or if we need help to hold our heads up. The simple answer is, "Be strong in the Lord and the power of His might." He put you there and will give you knowledge of who you are. That's where you gain your strength because you belong to God, and His hand is on you for this great and glorious assignment. I always tell myself if He didn't think I could do it, He would not have brought me to it. It's a hard assignment because sometimes it's inflexible. I would not be authentic if I didn't say there were times when I tried to change myself to fit in, whether it was in conversation or my style of dressing. However, I realized I was only making myself unhappy. But God came that I might have abundant life.

The Butterfly

When you try to do this assignment the way people want you to do it and not the way God is asking you to, believe me—it will always be a challenge. I remember one day teasing my husband about wanting me to do something how the people wanted me to do it. Yes, I tripped. I'm guilty of allowing people

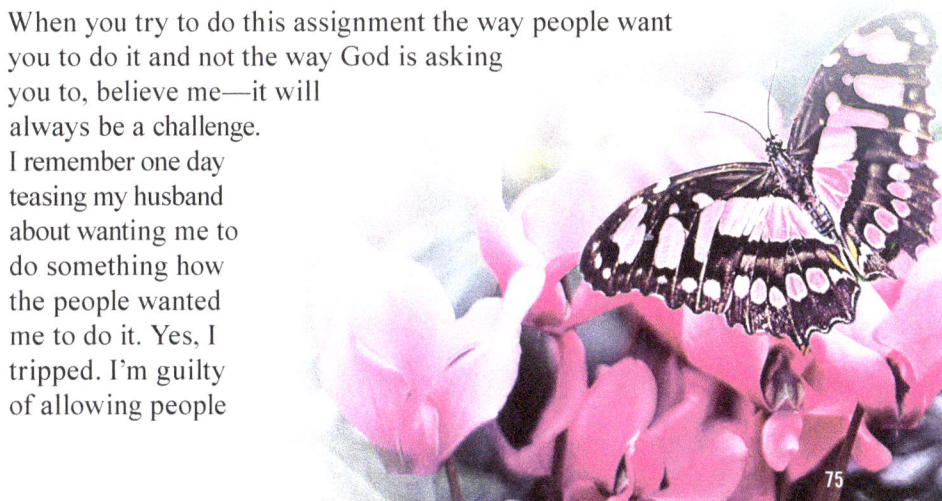

to make me feel I should do things the way they want me to, rather than what I feel in my heart. So, I started asking God, "Is this, okay? Should I do this? Should I say this? How will this work for me?" The more I sought His opinion, the easier it was to evolve into who He wanted me to be.

> In all thy ways acknowledge Him and He shall direct thy paths. (Proverbs 3:6)

So, like a caterpillar, I went through my own metamorphosis: egg, larva, pupa, and then adult. It's up to you what stage you want to stay at. As for me, I wanted to evolve into what I was intended to be. During the metamorphosis, the caterpillar's old body dies, and a new body takes form inside its protective shell or chrysalis. It is born with everything it needs to become a butterfly. It is the same with you; everything you need is already inside of you to become the beautiful queen and First Lady God has called you to be. God knows who you are.

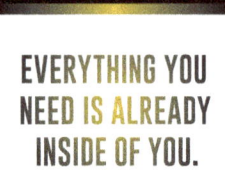
EVERYTHING YOU NEED IS ALREADY INSIDE OF YOU.

So, declare Psalm 139:14 over yourself: "I will praise you for I am fearfully and wonderfully made."

I went to a church service one night and as the visiting pastor got up to the podium to preach, he stopped suddenly, looked at me, and said these words, "I pray for First Ladies. You all have a hard job at times. I see most of you; you're like the Prego spaghetti sauce commercial says—'It's in there!'" I understood exactly what he meant. He was saying that everything I need was already in me. First Ladies, make sure you get your directions from God and watch Him work on your behalf.

What Is Your Niche?

In Genesis 2:18, God declared that it was not good for man to be alone, so He made a helper fit for him. The meaning of the word "helper" in Hebrew is "your husband's ideal partner; his unique complement." Adam needed a partner, someone to complete his life. You cannot be alone; you need a partner, too, and then you are in perfect unity. Celebrate your strengths together, the things that make you who you are, distinct from any other pastor's wife. One pastor's wife used to say, "I'm not a singer," but she was the most hospitable woman you'd ever meet. You couldn't beat her in the way she cared for and treated people. She was unmatched. That was her niche. What is your niche? What do you like and what don't you like? Be who God has made you to be, besides being beautiful and kind.

I'm a strong personality with a kind, giving heart. I can't be that First Lady who is quiet, and less talkative. On the other hand, some people say they wish they could express themselves the way I do. However, the way other First Ladies communicate with their congregations and their pastors/husbands works for them. Do what works for you. No one can beat you being you, not even on their best day. I've had the chance to watch many different First Ladies. I have a sister who was the pastor's wife whose mannerisms and personality made her beloved at her church. My sense of humor is what our congregation seems to like best about me, and that works for my ministry. The main thing is that I know who I am. Get to know who you are and really study the position and ministry of your church and be who God says you are.

NO ONE CAN BEAT YOU BEING YOU.

Position vs. Calling

A friend and I discussed whether being a First Lady is a calling or a position that she had married into. There's a big difference between position and calling. When it's a job, you do just enough to appease your husband and the people, but your heart is not wholeheartedly in it. You do what you do because you have to. But with a calling, you know without a shadow of a doubt the things you see, hear, and know will help make your church and your husband better because you have answered the call. You do what you do because you're happy and honored to be a part of the ministry.

Now, don't misunderstand me. Even with a calling, there can be times when you don't feel like doing it; you don't feel like smiling or being helpful. There are times when you don't feel like being the one people can count on all the time. Sometimes the members act as if no one else can sing as you sing; no one else can teach the way you do; no one can preach as you do. So, then you start to feel burned out! But there's something about that call that makes you muster up enough energy to continue doing what you do and keep it moving because it's a calling. You want to do whatever God has asked you to do.

At the same time, if you have your own ministry, there are places you still want to go. You still have your individual dreams and creative ideas that have nothing to do with the church. Your creative hands, spontaneous mind, gifts, and talents didn't just come because you are the pastor's wife; they are gifts and talents within you. They were already developed and a part of your life and who you were before you became a pastor's wife. God just put you into a called-out place called a "Pastors Wife" where you have the opportunity to use your gifts and talents.

You would know if you weren't called. First of all, you would not be able to withstand the trials and tribulations that come along with the position. When I say you withstand, it doesn't mean you don't cry, or your feelings don't get hurt. It doesn't mean you will love every moment because you will have those days. It's a call. So, you dust yourself off, square your shoulders, and "live to fight another day".

I salute First Ladies who don't get all the accolades and recognition that's due to them. I'm talking about you, First Ladies, who stand on the front line with your husbands. You see the attacks; you pray, and God changes the direction. When your husband talks, sometimes you want to intervene and tell him not to do this or that. But when he says, "The Lord told me to do it," you back off in humble submission because you trust the God in this man.

I wish I could say people don't look at us, and they aren't watching to see our reactions when our husbands say or do something we feel is inappropriate like getting after a leader in the ministry. An elect lady friend told me she wears hats to hide her face from the people and that it prevents them from pinpointing her thoughts. We are here for them but, most of all, we're here because we love God.

Queen Esther

People often think of Esther as being just one of the harem. But when Queen Vashti refused to present herself at the king's banquet, it opened the door for Esther to be chosen. Now, in Queen Vashti's defense, she didn't want to be made a public spectacle because she knew who she was. But there was a greater plan at work beyond her role. Therefore, God allowed her to be banished from the king's palace. Esther had absolutely no idea God would use her save a whole nation. But she obeyed her cousin, Mordecai, who heard from God.

We never know why we are in a situation. It is important to find out who you are and whose you are. Let God show you your personal mirror that reflects the image of everything He is: holy, righteous, pure, comforting, and loving. Let Him shape you into what you need to be for the people you serve.

I've had the privilege of knowing and serving under a few great examples and watching how these women maneuver their way around in ministry. When I say maneuver, it does not mean manipulate. They just knew how to go in and out among God's people. Esther had to be prepared for her role. She went through twelve months of preparation, training, and beauty treatments to make her look regal and win the king's heart. No wonder the king chose her out of all the women in his harem.

Your pastor, your husband, wanted you and if you're in this place for such a time as this, I believe it is God-ordained. This is a calling. If you take the time to really look at what it entails, recognize that your husband/pastor is a man after God's own heart. Why would God allow someone to walk with the man of God who does not appreciate his calling—or should I say—does not love and care for him?

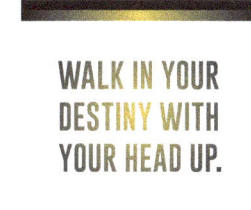

WALK IN YOUR DESTINY WITH YOUR HEAD UP.

Walk in your destiny with your head up. Everybody can't do what you're doing. Listen, whether you're a singer or an administrator, your husband's personal cheerleader or prayer warrior, it doesn't matter. You're there to assist the man of God; you're there to lift him up, to honor him in the eyes of the people. It's okay if you don't have many talents. What's important is who God thinks and believes you are, and how the man of God sees you. What matters is being the best you. No one can beat you at that. So, take care of yourself, truly love you. Loving yourself teaches others how they should treat you.

An Accessory?

First Ladies, can we talk? Remember who you are. Admittedly, people have called me some things that hurt me. A while back, I remember being referred to as an "accessory" when it came to my role as the pastor's wife. That bothered me. I was trying to figure out what that really meant. I was obedient like everyone else, gave my offering like everyone else, and worked in the church like everyone else.

First Ladies, Can We Talk?

I shared with another pastor's wife how being called an "accessory" made me feel. I began to cry as I listened to her tell me, "Sister, it'll be okay!" We talked a little bit longer and we got off the phone. A few hours later, I received a text message from her that said: "Sister, don't forget that accessories make outfits look good. Without the accessories, the outfit could be really plain. So, thank God that you are an accessory! Every ministry needs them." Have you ever looked at something and said, "Something's missing. Something doesn't look right"? Then you add the accessories, and it makes the outfit beautiful and complete. Well, if I'm an accessory, I'll be the prettiest, most accommodating accessory I can be. I texted her back and told her that her text message made me cry because it blessed me. "Wow, so he wears me well!" Be encouraged, elect ladies; smile when you want to smile and cry when you are down. Be who God has said you are. You didn't choose this. He chose you to be the best you can be in whatever ground you were planted. In that soil, there's going to be some dung, some stuff that doesn't feel good, but it helps us to grow.

I'm just sharing with you some of the experiences I've had before, during, and after my husband became a pastor. I looked at him one day with tears in my eyes, and I said these words from Psalm 119:71, "It was good for me to be afflicted that I might learn His statutes." At times, I thought this position was to kill and destroy me, but when I think about it, it has actually made me find out who God is. He is everything I need to help me be what He wants me to be. Every scar and tear is a badge of honor if you please God while going through trials.

There is a difference between complaining and stating your case in prayer. Complaining will hinder your prayer because it weakens your faith.

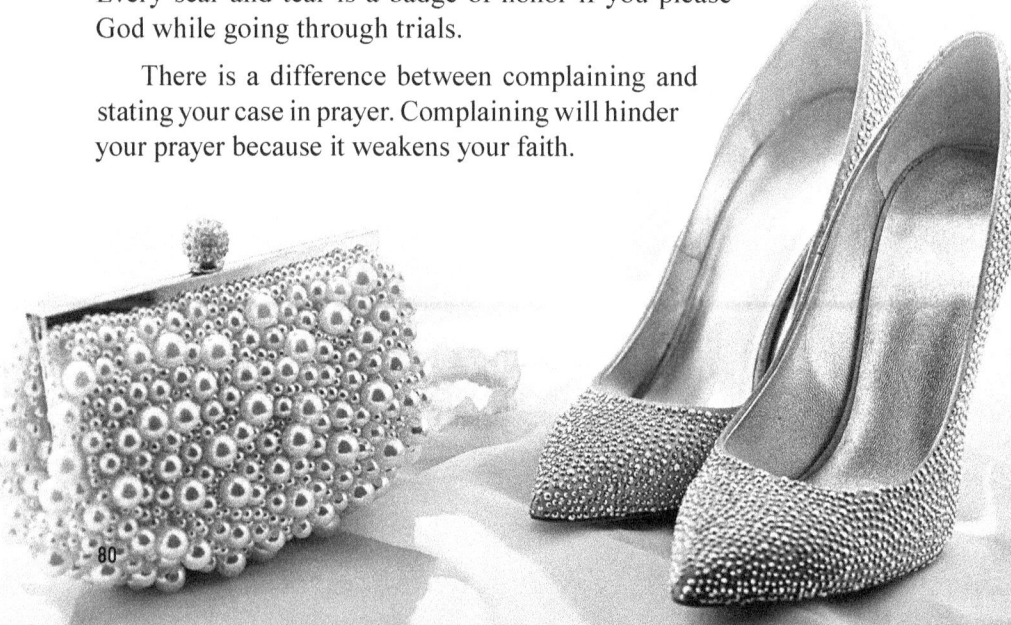

However, stating your case in prayer allows you to see what God is trying to work out in you or teach you. Second John 1:1-13 addresses the pastor's wife or elect lady, and it also tells all of us to be faithful unto death.

> And I will give thee the Crown of Life. (Revelation 2:10)

We must all work out our own salvation with fear and trembling (Philippians 2:12). God cares about every aspect of your life. Be encouraged. You're a beautiful accessory!

Suffering in Silence

Not every elect lady is doing fine, nor is every elect lady happy. I have met some who deal with psychological, mental, and, yes, physical abuse, through my knowledge as CEO of a nonprofit called No Hands Lifted. Abuse comes in so many forms. Many women, ranging from the wives of pastors, doctors, and lawyers, you name it, suffer in silence and for many different reasons. In their silence, they lose the essence of who they are, why they are, and even what their goals are for themselves. Even though a lot of these women have never been physically abused, they say to me, "I'd rather if he hit me than say the things he says to me, things that I can't ever get over or even get out of my head."

Women of God let's look out for one another. Let's not only recognize when we're hurt, sad, or depressed, but also see and hear the cries of other elect ladies. When I speak of these women being psychologically or physically abused, I never refer to their husbands as being men of God because a true man of God will not hit, fight, or harm his wife. Sometimes First Ladies are neglected because their husbands/pastors are so busy trying to help solve problems and issues of the people in the ministry. There are good pastors who have not mastered the art of saying no to people or taking a rest. These men sometimes neglect the simple things their wives need like her husband's time.

I have friends whose husbands are pastors in different Reformations. They make sure their husbands go on vacation three times a year. They make sure they are well taken care of because they understand the mantle over their lives. They also understand their responsibilities as elect ladies to keep their husbands strong, happy, and fit to be the pastors they need.

If you know any woman who needs help due to domestic violence, please ask her to call the National Domestic Violence Hotline (800) 799-7233.

Don't be ashamed, even if it's you. First Lady, can we talk? Part of who you are is not only how you have been taken care of by your husband but how you view yourself. Some may even ask, "What is my responsibility?" The people who know their God shall do exploits—extraordinary things for God. Who are you in God's eyes? You are powerful; you are strong; you can do exceedingly abundantly above all that you could ask or think according to the power that lies within you. You are fit for the battle. You are equipped with God when you know what He is doing or intends to do in your life. Do you believe you are who God says you are?

IF ANY WOMAN NEEDS HELP, ASK HER TO CALL THE HOTLINE.

PRAYER

Dear Father, You make us look at life from a beautiful and promising perspective. We are not defeated and will not give in to defeat. Your Word is a sustained presence and a light in days of darkness and insecurity. Thank You that we as women of God can depend on You, daily. Even when we can't quite see what You are doing, we know You are with us. We may not be able to speak to anyone, but we can always share our thoughts and hearts with You. Thank You for seeing the secret parts of us! Our bodies belong to You, for we are the temples of the Lord. We declare Your protection and guidance over our lives and all those in our care. In Jesus' name. Amen.

WRITE YOUR AFFIRMATION OF CONFIDENCE

CHAPTER 7

WHEN THE BOUGH BREAKS

> Strive for peace with everyone, and for the holiness without which no one will see the Lord. (Hebrew 12:14 ESV)

We all know this nursery rhyme and have sung it to our children:

> *Rock a bye baby on the treetop.*
>
> *When the wind blows the cradle will rock.*
>
> *When the bough breaks the cradle will fall.*
>
> *And down will come baby, cradle, and all.*

Members have left our church and honestly, I said, "Whew! Thank You, Lord, they needed to leave!" They were troublemakers, and they sowed seeds of discord. As spiritual parents, one of the most painful things to experience is when the children whom you've poured your time, your dime, and your talents into leave you. It is one thing to watch them grow and leave because they are starting a ministry or something like that, but when you hear they are leaving because they are going to another ministry—to be transparent—it hurts! We have never cried, but the loss on our investment has been great. There's nothing worse than watching members who edify the body leave, and you don't know why.

This may seem harsh, but I have learned to put people into two categories: assets and liabilities. They are assets when they attend services regularly, help support the ministry financially and participate in nurturing the church body and community. They don't complain and truly want the body of Christ to grow. These people help build the kingdom! On the other hand, there are those who, though they have a firm foundation in Christ, are solid liabilities. They attend services when it's convenient for them, or when it fits into their schedule. They are not consistent supporters of the ministry, but they are the neediest. Now, don't get me wrong; I believe in giving help, but there comes a time when the recipient can give something more than money—and that's their precious time.

We love our children and want the best for them but what can you do when they are grown and feel they can make it on their own? You watch and pray. We are not built to carry anyone's burdens but our own. We are not God! Galatians 6:5 says, "For every man shall bear his burden." Having eight children, you learn their different personalities, who they are individually, and provide the level of support they each need accordingly. Even when it's not always reciprocated.

Forgiveness vs. Reconciliation

One thing that can break the bough is a misunderstanding between church members and leadership. Proverbs 4:7 urges us, "In all thy getting get understanding." As a pastor's wife, you try to figure out so many times what you said or did to offend others. You wonder if your facial expressions caused someone to feel offended. Even when you don't understand, you must forgive without question. I have found out through the years that forgiveness is what God requires unconditionally. There's no way you can keep moving through the daily interactions, committee meetings, and so forth without forgiveness. Things will be said and done at times that you will have to come to grips with. You will have to realize that at the end of the day, all you can do is forgive as God forgives.

I've come to understand the difference between forgiveness and reconciliation. In Rick Warren's book, *The Purpose Driven Life,* he lets us know that "Forgiveness is a must, but trust must be earned for a person to fully bring you back into reconciliation." Sometimes forgiveness is a process but it's necessary. If we don't forgive, God will not forgive us. I know if I did not have the power of the Holy Ghost, I would surely have missed God at times.

Peter asked Jesus how many times he should forgive his brother. Jesus simply told him, "seventy times seven." Forgiveness will keep you alive! while unforgiveness eats at you like cancer. There have been times when I wanted to walk down the other side of the aisle at church because of a hostile gaze. But when true forgiveness happens, you know it; you recognize it, and you feel it because the sting of what was done to you is no longer there. You can face people and look them in the eye. That doesn't mean you have to go to lunch with them, but the fact that you forgave keeps your line free, clears your mind, and keeps your soul intact. Without forgiveness, the bough will break. Hurts, offenses, and misfired words will happen, so we must guard our hearts and minds.

UNFORGIVENESS EATS AT YOU LIKE CANCER.

I remember a comment that was made by Pastor Marvin Sapp as he addressed the National Apostolic convention. He said, "Love the people but don't fall in love with them." I thought that was a little strange for a man of God to say until I experienced some bough-breaking moments. Then I understood I had to still love people because the Word of God says, we owe no man anything but love. What the "fall in love" expression implies here, is that when these unforeseen events happen, if you're not covered in the blood, you can be hurt to the core.

This Is Ministry

First Ladies have told me there were misunderstandings in their churches and ministries that broke them so much they could hardly lift their heads. They didn't want to go back to church or work in the ministry because everybody took the side of the other people, and no one understood them.

This is ministry. When you understand that it's ministry, and you see the bough break, you must remember your goal is to serve God and keep your husband and family safe. You do this mainly through prayer. I heard a bishop say that no one wants to lose any members, bad ones, or good ones, and that's true! But I'd rather people go where they can serve and be great members, than stay and poison others because they don't really want to be there. I've seen pastors cry because people they really depended on, who they thought would never leave, left their ministries.

That's what I want to say to you, First Ladies, elect ladies: the bough will break at some point in your ministry. But take in the moments when people tell you they appreciate the work you and your husband do, and the times when they show you they're glad they serve under your leadership, when they are grateful for the advice given, and the times you prayed for them and their families. Take it in because the bough will one day break; that's inevitable. But what is more constant is the grace, mercy, and love of God during these hard times. You'll feel His arms embrace you. You'll hear Him say to you, "It's going to be okay!" I've seen people leave and I didn't think we would ever recover. But soon after they left, we looked up and new people came who were profitable to the ministry and helped build and nurture it. So, First Lady, be encouraged and encourage your husband and children to stay focused. Remember, it's ministry.

Family Ties

I belong to a church that my husband's family also attends. I guess I'm one of the blessed ones because they don't interfere with his decisions or give directions to our ministry. On the other hand, some pastors say to me, "I wish my sister would leave. I wish my mom would be quiet. I dislike my brother being here" because when they get mad at them, they are disrespectful. They forget who the pastor is and treat him like the younger brother. One pastor told me of the time he had to go to his sister and ask her to leave because she was poisoning the members by telling them things she did not like about the ministry. He would share with the members the direction God had given him for the ministry and his sister would tell them they didn't have to follow it. That's a bough-breaking moment.

We may think people don't watch our family members, but they do, and they even get direction from them. My husband's siblings respect him because he lives a life of prayer and holiness. His siblings are connected to the body enough to know that when he's at church, he's not just their brother, but he is also walking in the office of their pastor, and they honor that God-given position.

Even if I don't always agree with some of the decisions my husband makes, I have enough sense to know he's a strong man. I am the one God put in a supportive position and a threefold cord is not easily broken. I don't want to disarm him in front of the people. I want to keep him lifted because if I lose confidence and the congregation sees it, they too will lose confidence. I don't want to be part of that bough that breaks. I have private conversations with my husband when I don't understand, and I'm appreciative of him allowing me to ask those questions. But I always make it clear that, whatever he decides, I will follow because I believe in the God in him.

Lights, Camera, Action

People can be fickle-minded. Do you remember the people who greeted Jesus as He rode into town on the colt? One day they were saying, "Hosanna! Hosanna!" and the next day they were saying, "Crucify Him! Crucify Him!" You will never have problems with some people; they have a genuine concern for you, your family, and the ministry. Then there will be some who don't care why they're there. They just needed a place to land and, unfortunately, they landed with you.

Church members come in categories. The first is the steadfast category. These are the ones who won't leave the ministry no matter what. They support the church with their time, tithes, and talents. They're steadfast, unmovable, always abounding in the work of the Lord. These are the best members to have! You can count on them to be on time, accountable, and faithful, not just to the ministry but also to God.

Then you have fair-weather members, who literally depend on the season. If it's raining, they may not make it. If it's summer, it might be too hot. If it's winter, it's too cold. If it's spring they're planting their gardens. You don't see much of them at all, but they are still members.

Then you have the holiday members—Easter, Christmas, baptisms, church anniversaries, and pastor's business meetings. We call these members, "Lights, Camera, Action," but we are still called to love them. I guess no matter who you have in your church, it's up to you to do your part, and that is to love them until God finds them or they find God when the bough breaks.

In 2019, we were hit with the loss of two prominent families. Now, the church will always manage; it doesn't come to a halt because it's God's church and His people. But I watched my husband promote and give many ministry opportunities to one of these families. After that, they told us God said it was time for them to leave. I asked the pastor,

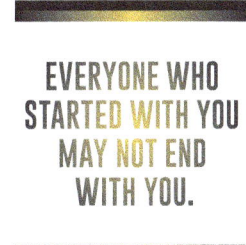

EVERYONE WHO STARTED WITH YOU MAY NOT END WITH YOU.

my husband, why he felt so bad, and he said, "It makes you feel so rejected as if they're saying, "You're not good enough and could have done things differently." At the same time, I believe God sends us people who we need at the right moment. Any time anyone leaves, it allows others to grow and expand. Everyone who started with you may not end with you.

I rebuke the spirit of rejection off the men and women of God. The spirit of rejection victimizes us and makes us feel worthless and unwanted. I believe when people are called to a ministry, they will help the ministry to prosper; they will not talk against it or tear it down. Faithfulness is more than being dutiful in your post. It's also being present with the attitude of "Let this mind be in you which was also in Christ Jesus." This speaks of their attitude: when they are faithful, everyone can feel it. In general, every leader need's people who are committed to tithing, available, and prayerful. If you pray and ask God for clear directions, even when the bough breaks, you are prepared.

In our denomination, we have what is called a Pastor and Wife Appreciation. This is an annual event where the congregation showers their pastors and their wives with monetary gifts and words of appreciation. They sit you down for two or three days and designated church members are provided the opportunity to get up and say nice things about you. Other churches are invited to come to enjoy the celebratory event. I look forward to these appreciation events, but I am always apprehensive when I hear people say, "I'm here to stay. I'm not going anywhere" because they are sure to leave within a few months. I've learned to sit and smile and stay in the moment, even when someone leaves our ministry. We take it in stride now. We focus on the people who stay and love on them. When you realize what you are doing and who you're doing it for, you are reminded that only what you do for Christ will last.

In the 90s I was involved in a house fire. Fortunately, no one was hurt. But this thought crossed my mind: when a pastor loses a member of his church, it's like a fire ignited in the spiritual house. If it were a real fire, we would tell them to stop, drop, and roll. You stop to assess the situation. You drop on your knees to ask God what's next, and you roll and keep it moving.

PRAYER

Father, we enjoy oneness with You. We are complete with no one. When feelings of rejection, jealousy, strife, or indecisiveness enter, our calm and correction are in You. We will refer to and yield to Your Word. Our commitment is to become better, stronger, and wiser. Father, we love Your people. We realize it is about pleasing and serving so that You will get all the glory. It is not about us. Help us to understand what the bigger picture is. As women of God, we will flow and move in You. In Jesus' name. Amen.

WRITE YOUR AFFIRMATION OF ONENESS

_____

_____

_____

_____

_____

_____

_____

_____

_____

CHAPTER 8

WHAT ABOUT THE CHILDREN?

Lo, children are an heritage of the Lord: and the fruit of the womb is his reward. (Psalm 127:3)

Growing up, I never wanted to disappoint my parents and always felt accepted. As a parent, I consistently need to reassure my children they are loved and appreciated. People will come and go, but our children, who are laboring with us in the ministry, need to know they are important to us, even when they make mistakes. Our children are not exempt from painful heartaches and disappointments. However, it doesn't mean we compromise because of their mistakes. Remember the mistakes we made and got away with. We love our children, encourage them to have a personal relationship with God, and teach them to love themselves.

Both my husband and I were born into ministry. Both of our parents were pastors and lived devout Christian lives before us. They were genuinely God-fearing people. We came from the same denomination with the same values and ways of thinking regarding spiritual disciplines. Yet, through all our similarities, we were very different. The differences were in our parent's structuring styles. During those times, our denomination was very strict, and there were a lot of dos and don'ts, rules, and regulations. Sometimes these differences can present challenges. My husband's upbringing was more confined within the church structure; my upbringing was a little more lenient. I recall my siblings and I being allowed to wear gym clothes and swimsuits, whereas some were not allowed to wear certain clothing;

First Ladies, Can We Talk?

we watched secular music programs such as *American Bandstand* and *Soul Train*. Can any of you relate to any of this in your household?

My husband's church schedule was different than mine. When we were children, my siblings and I could ask my parents if we could stay home from church because of homework and school assignments, and they would allow us to do so. Both of our parents allowed us to be who we needed to be in God. Our mutual respect for our upbringing helped my husband and I fall in love with God and kingdom work.

Our denomination was also known for attending service five-days a week which is what my husband experienced. However, our family went on Wednesday night for youth and Friday for family night. We both experienced attending service all day Sunday. Yet both families were filled with love and laughter. I'm speaking about differences, not parenting. We must know the difference; it's essential. Everybody's home is different, and we must respect that.

I'm grateful for my husband's upbringing, as it was similar to mine, but the differences required much compromising for us to merge as one. I wanted a good marriage, and I desired for our blended family to be united. We both learned to compromise, see the other side, and sometimes agree to disagree respectfully. However, we're not disagreeable and never seek to hurt or make each other look bad in anyone else's eyes.

What About the Children?

Our families were important to our fathers. My father wanted us to be involved in every aspect of his life. He wanted us to love God, work in the church, and build ourselves up in our most holy faith, praying in the Holy Ghost. To this day, I still teach, sing a little, and play the piano a little bit to help if needed because, as a young girl, my father encouraged me to do the will of God. Let me encourage you to invite balance into your home with your children and your husband.

Your Family Is Paramount

Out of my eight children, one of my sons, Kristopher, plays the keyboard, drums, and bass. My son, Isaiah, plays the drums, and my son, Tyler, plays the guitar. My son, Ja'Briane, is in a choral group. Marcus plays the drums. Jhamond works in the sound booth. He also plays the drums and the organ sometimes. My daughters, Chara and Cherael, and Jaya (our bonus daughter) are outstanding singers. All my children work in some area of the ministry, and it wasn't forced on them. The truth is, sometimes, they would ask if they could attend church. But that bitter taste of church is not in any of them—at least, they haven't said so. I support my husband, my friend, but I also understand I cannot be everything people desire of me. First and foremost, I'm a wife, a mother, and then a pastor's wife.

I appreciate my husband for letting it be known he is not married to the church—he's married to me! The church is the third entity in our lives, so the order is God, family, and church. Nurture your family; love your children; love each other because people come and go. Your children and spouse should be paramount in your life. The church is the bride of Christ.

Don't let the church become your be-all-and-end-all. Don't let the church people become your entire life. Your life is your family, and your goal is always to please God.

I remember a pastor friend of ours who allowed his son to be chastised by a stranger in front of a whole group of people. Since that day, we haven't seen that young man in the church. Protect your children. I don't mean with a strong arm or to disrespect others, but you must get to the meat of the matter.

My father never ever just took the word of people when they said I did something wrong. He knew Leisa had an attitude and Leisa had some problems but even so, my father would always seek the truth. He would not just believe what he heard from members. My father and mother were the advocates for our family. I'm grateful for how much they protected and looked out for us.

I remember a lady in our church who was not happy that I was friends with her daughter. One day, she did something very upsetting to me. She thought I had on lipstick (which we were not allowed to wear back then), but it was really a little lip gloss. This woman was cruel and unkind. Standing next to the restroom at church, she walked over to me and harshly wiped my lips with a Kleenex. When she saw the little lip gloss on the Kleenex, she rolled her eyes and walked off. I should have told my father!

Then there was another occasion when a member complained about my siblings and me singing in the choir and doing too much in the church. My father let it be known, "Before we let you abuse and mistreat our children, I will let them go down the street to another church where they can be used in ministry! Our children need to work out their own soul's salvation just like yours." My parents didn't have much of a problem after that.

Some people will get close to your children to actually try to find out how you live, what you do, what you say, where you go, and even what you eat. Protect your children. Let them know in no uncertain terms not to give in to prying eyes, and their home life is important. My children said something to me I'll never forget. They said, "This is the only place we can be who we are, where we can laugh and talk and say what we want to say without anyone judging us and making us feel bad."

My husband did that for me and our children, and I'm so appreciative to this day that we never had to walk on eggshells in our home. Our children were allowed to be themselves and those who entered our home were welcomed to be themselves too. My children love God and what He stands for. I had family devotions with my children when they were young. I was a stay-at-home mom at the time, and my husband wasn't a pastor yet. I'd sit on the couch and sing a little song:

Ain't it a wonder about Jesus,

He's a wonder in my soul...

When I sang, my kids would come from their rooms, the kitchen, and outside because my voice would carry. They would get on their knees around me one by one to sing with me. I'd add a little prayer for God to protect and watch over us. I would listen to them tell God how they loved Him, and how He helped them in school. When conflicts and things that bothered them crept up, I would teach them to pray and know who to lean on in times of trouble. When they grew up, they remembered the times spent learning who God is. They remember me teaching, praying, and crying with them. I know the scripture, "Train up a child in the way he should go and when he is old, he will not depart from it." That's talking about training them up for life, how to take care of themselves, how to be self-sufficient, how to manage their lives, and not just training in the church.

I got my training from my parents. They taught my siblings and me how to pray. Mom could pray for hours. I remember going with her to noonday prayer when I was only 12 years old. The best thing we can give our children is the knowledge of God. By the time they're adults, you can no longer guide them;

I GOT MY TRAINING FROM MY PARENTS.

in fact, they will no longer even accept your wise counsel. I can honestly say I was twenty-three when I really got to know who God was. I was alone by myself in Germany when I got to know God for myself, and not just the God of my mother and father. Parents, teach your children to get to know God and to love and serve Him.

I admire Bishop T.D. Jakes and his daughters for how they learned to love God of their own volition, without being coerced. I can only hope and pray for the same thing for my sons. I hope one day, God will bring them close. When your children reach adulthood, they will always be your children, so make sure they have a positive and loving image of God. One thing my parents never did was speak negative, nasty, or disrespectful words about the people who served under their ministry. This is how I tried to bring up my children as well. If someone hurt them, I would tell them to let me know, and let me deal with it. One of the hardest things to do is to not slip and say something nasty in front of your children about a sister or brother, or whoever is harming your children.

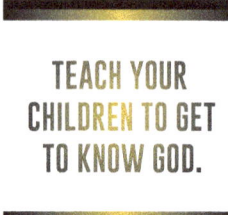

TEACH YOUR CHILDREN TO GET TO KNOW GOD.

You must be true in your heart because your children know you when the church people don't. I adopted what I saw my parents do for my sisters, brother, and me. They looked to see our God-given talents and helped us to develop our gifts. Don't forget your children; they too must work out their own salvation. Even if they stray, let it be said you gave them a firm foundation. You gave them God!

PRAYER

Our children are gifts from the Father. As mothers, we are to be good stewards of our seeds. We declare their future is bright and they love the Lord with all their hearts. They are protected and will do great exploits in your name so people will see their good works and glorify the Father. We ask You, Father, that they will make You first in all they do and strive to become. Satan, the blood of Jesus is against you! No hurt, harm, or danger shall come near them. They will love the Lord and tell their friends of God's goodness and mercy. Father, we pray that they walk following the Word. They will not be ashamed of the gospel of Jesus Christ. Our children are blessed and will not conform to the world's system. In Jesus' name. Amen.

WRITE YOUR AFFIRMATION OF FAMILY SUCCESS

CHAPTER 9

FIRST LADIES SPEAK

> The aged women likewise, that they be in behaviour as becometh holiness, not false accusers, not given to much wine, teachers of good things; That they may teach the young women to be sober, to love their husbands, to love their children, to be discreet, chaste, keepers at home, good, obedient to their own husbands, that the word of God be not blasphemed. (Titus 2:3-5)

I had the opportunity to interview some of my First Lady friends, and I asked them a few questions. The following are the questions I asked them and their responses:

Question One: What is the best thing about being the First Lady?

"Walking in ministry with my husband, supporting him, and working on my salvation is what I enjoy."

Question Two: How do you solve conflict?

"Through the Word and discernment. You need God's guidance because you can't take sides. You must allow the people to see you are praying and asking God what to do and say. You must discuss issues, if necessary."

Question Three: What regrets, if any, do you have?

"I have no regrets. I had to be available all the time; I had to be there if no one else showed up. "Being a pastor's wife is easy because he allows me to have a voice in the ministry; however, ours is a small ministry and I wear a lot of hats—and this can wear you out." —AK

"If I had any regrets, it would be that sometimes the pastors have no accountability and there is no mentorship for young pastors who are just starting." —RR

Question Four: Is being a pastor a calling or are you born into it?

"It is a calling. Your mother and grandmother could be elect ladies, but you must be called to this because the same passion your husband has falls upon you. Maybe it's not to be a speaker but to do ministry and to help in the ministry. You can't do it without God's help and the call placed upon your life. I will never say that I know it all or that I'm the only one who has gone through and understands everything."

And I'm sure we can all benefit from a few insights of former First Lady's whose husbands have passed or retired. Their identities will be kept undisclosed to protect their congregations, their husbands, and themselves. The following are their responses:

Question One: What is the best thing about being the First Lady?

"The best thing about being the First Lady is being entrusted by God to serve His people. Second, it's being identified by the parishioners to serve them, and lastly, being anointed by God to serve alongside my husband. I didn't marry a pastor; I married a military man. However, many years later, the Lord called my husband into the ministry. Oh, my God, that meant I would be the pastor's wife and that our children would be pastor's kids!

"Certain difficulties come with the territory, but it was more of a blessing than a burden. The respect and love showed to you, the pastor's wife, by the church members is a great blessing. Some members go out of their way to make the pastor's wife's life a positive experience. For the pastor's wife, friendships in the church are hard to cultivate; however, God allows specific individuals to primarily serve alongside you. They are considered confidantes and are entrusted by God with your care. Often, these individuals in the church are called adjutants. They add to your life a presence, responsibility, and concern, and guard your heart at all costs.

"In the Bible, Jonathan, King David's beloved friend, always loyal to the anointed David, could be considered an adjutant (see 1 Samuel 20:1-42). Adjutants understand your calling; they allow you to be your own person and have your own identity. The love of the saints, the support of the mothers in Zion who are always hugging you, kissing you, and encouraging you, and the visible love of your pastor/husband are other great advantages of being the First Lady." —Lady H.V.

"At our church, the previous First Lady remained in that position after her husband died, and I thought, oh boy, this was going to be hard. It turned out that having her as a spiritual mentor was the best thing I could ever have asked for. Her advice as an experienced pastor's wife and her positive and wholesome words were invaluable. At the same time, mostly, the wisdom she shared kept any mistakes I made as a pastor's wife to a minimum."

"Lastly, the love of the children toward me as the pastor's wife was beyond amazing. The children would always make me something, always draw me a picture or a card, and often threw me kisses. That gave me so much joy. There is a price to service and servitude, for didn't Jesus Himself say:"

> If you insist on saving your life, you will lose it. Only those who throw away their lives for my sake and for the sake of the Good News will ever know what it means to really live. (Mark 8:35 TLB)

"Being the First Lady is a gift from God with many demands, but you must know who you are in Christ Jesus and focus your service on Him. The following scripture is a life verse for me:"

> That I may know him, and the power of his resurrection, and the fellowship of his sufferings.
> (Philippians 3:10a NKJV)

"As a First Lady, you might experience a gamut of emotions ranging from bountiful blessings to profound betrayals as you serve in the kingdom. Knowing who you are, having a clear definition of your purpose, fortifying yourself through a powerful prayer life, and attempting to have a well-balanced personal life, help you experience the joy of being a First Lady."

When First Lady S.R spoke to me, she told me about her troubled marriage. She was a First Lady for ten years. Here's what she had to share:

"Many years went by as I continued to pray for change. What I didn't know was how things were going to change. I covered, protected, smiled, and served in ministry because ultimately, that was my life.

"When it came to my home life and the church, I learned how to separate the two. But the day came when I could no longer hide the pain on my face. One Sunday, I left the service before my husband mounted the pulpit to preach. During that time, my youngest daughter wasn't quite a year old yet, so it was the perfect excuse for me to slip out of the church. That fake smile on my face was pathetic. For me, that was huge because I love to laugh, and when I'm sad, it's laughter that helps to pull me out of a low place. I love people, but things were very bad at home, and it felt as if everybody knew it, and, in some weird way, the church members were turning on me. But I realized much later that was mostly due to my own internal disconnection that was evolving because of the turmoil in my marriage.

"I loved my husband/pastor, but I didn't know then what I know now. We were young when he began to pastor our ministry, and I admit I was terrified. It never looked glamorous or anything that I'd ever want any husband of mine to do.

"My dad was a pastor, and growing up, I had already seen how that calling could interfere, even with my mother and father's good relationship. But the responsibility of leading God's people—who can love you today, not like you tomorrow, be easily offended by this or that, leave your church to go join another, and then talk about your ministry and what was lacking after they left—was great, even when it wasn't much appreciated. Through my challenges as a pastor's wife, I've experienced abuse, betrayal, lies, character assassination, and feeling like an outcast, unwanted, and unloved.

"As the years went by, I felt as if I was living with a total stranger who I never knew, and, sadly, he treated me like he never knew me either—as if I had never given him a child. I didn't know at the time what the total outcome of our marriage would be. I had an idea, but I was afraid because everything would change—and what would that look like? What was that going to mean for me? Unfortunately, but necessary for me, it meant divorce. For years, I remained silent about things I should have shared and even gotten counseling about.

"He wasn't accountable to anyone. I covered and protected him before the eyes of the people, and now he was the man on stage with a mic in hand to smear my name in front of anyone who would listen. I cried, and I cried because I felt God had left me all alone. How could He have allowed this to happen to me? I dealt with so many emotions. I blamed myself time and time again wondering why I didn't say anything. I was angry because I had sacrificed a lot, and I had given a lot and now everything was destroyed—or so I thought. But God! I feel praise down on the inside. "I'm Thanking God I'm fine and all is well.

Jehovah Shalom

From all the experiences shared by these First Ladies, I would say with a clear conscience that an elect lady cannot do this job without Jehovah Shalom. Have you ever needed the peace of God? We all need it. I will admit that I need His peace all the time. Let's do a quick background on how Jehovah Shalom came to be one of the names of God.

"Jehovah Shalom" was first mentioned in Judges Chapter 6. The children of Israel were being oppressed by the Midianites, not only them, but the Amalekites as well. But Judges 6:1 lets us know that the children of Israel were worshiping idols and doing ungodly things in the sight of God. The Bible says God allowed them to be harassed for seven years. When they planted their seeds, the Midianites would come and destroy their crops. They would also take their sheep, oxen, and donkeys, leaving them with nothing to eat.

When the children of Israel were reduced to poverty, only then would they cry out to the Lord for help. They knew the only one to turn to was the God of their fathers. Then God would discipline them, they would repent, and God would deliver them. But they would again find themselves in rebellion. It was the same cycle over and over again because they acted according to their own moral code:

In those days there was no king in Israel: every man did that which was right in his own eyes.
　　　　(Judges 21:45)

No wonder they had no peace! Whenever you are not in the will of God and you disobey Him, you will have no peace.

This was the background for when the angel of the Lord appeared to Gideon in Ophrah. Gideon was threshing wheat in the winepress. Let me stop right here. When they threshed wheat, they had to be at an elevated place like a hill. They would beat the wheat, so the heavier grain would drop to the bottom, while the unwanted chaff would blow away in the wind. They needed to be elevated—Lord, elevate us! One of our problems is we need to go higher in God to get our peace. Elevate Him so your peace can reach you.

Well, you can see at once from Gideon threshing wheat in the winepress that he was in the wrong place. It was the right thing for him to be threshing the wheat, but this was not the place to be doing it. How many times have you been in the wrong place, doing the right thing? You think you are helping but you are not helping at all. You find yourself forfeiting your peace for the sake of other people, places, or things, or you can be where you're supposed to be, but still not be functioning in the will of God. So, you still have no peace.

Just like Gideon in the winepress, hiding from the Midianites, I have found myself hiding at times, not because of shame but to regroup. In this walk, you may need to regroup and get a new strategy. How many times have we been in the wrong place? But God can still find us.

When the angel of the Lord appeared to Gideon, he addressed him as, "Mighty man of valor, the Lord is with you." Do you see how God always calls out our potential? Gideon answered, "If God is with me, then why are we in this horrible situation? We need the God of our fathers who delivered us from the Egyptians!" Women of God, we sometimes get it twisted just like Gideon did. We all have crosses we must take up daily and follow Christ. What makes our crosses seem hard to bear is when we try to carry them, along with other people's crosses. We cannot do both. Help us, Lord! But I'm here to tell you that God will give you peace amid every storm.

We cannot maneuver things the way we want. We need God's peace to lead, guide and direct us. We need it today! God, we need Your peace! Gideon forgot about the sins of the people that had brought their suffering upon them but because of their cry, God delivered them again. You too can cry out to God—He wants to help you! When Gideon realized it was an angel, he was afraid and began to tell God how inadequate he was:

"I am the least of my clan and am not worthy." No, you are what God declares you to be and God says to you, "You are the man and woman I have called to shepherd My sheep!"

Gideon then built an altar and called it Jehovah Shalom, "The Lord is Peace" (Judges 6:24). Jehovah is the name God gave Himself in Exodus 3:14: "I AM THAT I AM," which is Yahweh or Jehovah, the self-revealing God. This same God initiates a relationship with us. Here's how we should respond: "Jehovah Shalom, I need Your peace, harmony, wholeness, completeness, and tranquility. I need the absence of strife, envy, jealousy, and hate."

Dr. Tony Evans said, "God is the one who brings calm where there is chaos and stability where there is a struggle. Sin disrupts our peace, so we must keep our lives clear of it. It's the only thing that will keep God from intervening on our behalf." Jehovah Shalom wants to give us peace that surpasses all understanding. Isaiah 26:3 says, "Thou will keep him in perfect peace whose mind is stayed on him: because he trusts in him." The peace I'm talking about will keep your mind intact when everything around you seems to be crazy. The battlefield for your peace is in the mind because the Devil wants to destroy your peace.

> **THE BATTLEFIELD FOR YOUR PEACE IS IN THE MIND.**

Those who live according to the flesh have their minds set on what the flesh desires; but those who live in accordance with the Spirit have their minds set on what the Spirit desires. The mind governed by the flesh is death, but the mind governed by the Spirit is life and peace. Now the mind of the flesh is death but the mind of the spirit is life and peace. (Romans 8:5-6 NIV)

This is the spiritual well-being that comes from walking with God. God's peace is like no other. It can go where you can't go. He is the God of peace, your shelter in the storm. He's the God of peace who sends shalom for your depression, shalom for your oppression, shalom for your anxiety, shalom for your children, and shalom for your wayward thoughts. He sends peace to the troubled mind. The ultimate peace is peace with God:

> Peace, I leave with you, My peace I give to you; not as the world gives do I give to you. (John 14:27 NKJV)

I need and want the peace of God. The Jewish people say shalom for hello and goodbye. We too need Jehovah Shalom when we are coming in and when we are going out.

PRAYER

At times, we may feel alone and forsaken, but God, You are with us. You are the God of peace and harmony. Thank You, Lord, for being a great God. When we can't remember what to say, we can call upon Jesus. The name of Jesus is higher than any other name. Thank You, Lord, for life in You. Thank You for Your protection against every foul spirit and demonic presence. We are safe and secure. You are the God of all. We honor You! In Jesus' name. Amen.

WRITE YOUR AFFIRMATION OF WHO GOD IS TO YOU

_____

_____

_____

_____

_____

_____

_____

_____

CHAPTER 10

WIFE OF THE PASTOR OR THE PASTOR'S WIFE?

House and riches are the inheritance of fathers: and a prudent wife is from the Lord. (Proverbs 19:14)

I was once asked, "Are you a pastor's wife or the wife of the pastor?" I believe there is a difference. The pastor's wife is in full ministry with her husband; they are a team. On the other hand, the wife of the pastor deals strictly with the pastor's concerns. Some pastors whose wives have passed say, "They want a wife for them, not for the ministry." If this is wrong, I'm not one to say to fit into either category. It is up to the pastor and his wife.

I've also seen where the pastor's wife has more leeway and say in the decision-making for the direction of their church because the pastor feels she's a vital part of the ministry team. Her cooperation is needed, and the people watching her know that she will be his backup, pusher, and support. She's also, from what I see, a workhorse! Sometimes she becomes a little frustrated when he allows her to work without opening her mouth and giving her input. She gets tired, but what makes it okay is if he recognizes the ministry in her. He also realizes when she needs time to take a break and regroup.

Let me make this clear. Not every pastor's wife wants to be upfront, to be the one singing in the choir, or giving directions. I'm talking to the First Lady who is out there in the front. First Ladies in this calling have often told me there are not enough people to fill the various positions in the ministry, especially if the church is small and hasn't grown to the capacity you pray it will.

Learn to Delegate

At the same time, some of you won't let it grow any larger. You won't take your hands off that assignment and give someone else a chance to develop and grow. One of the most incredible things a pastor's wife could do is to work herself out of a position. What I mean by that is when you take the time to train others and provide the opportunity for them to learn and develop their ministries, you can sit back and watch the fruit of your labor as you move into the next phase of your ministry.

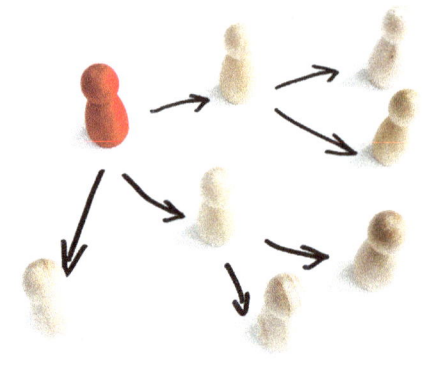

I've always worked in whatever position my pastor wants me to be in. I don't go ahead of our pastor. He is sovereign, so he prayerfully appoints people in places he feels will work best for their personalities and the ministry.

I watched my mother work in ministry and help train and develop other people. You can't be everything to everyone; you can't do it all. Sometimes you must take a break and sit back. You must assess who can do that ministry. Now, I'm not the greatest singer, so I get those who can sing to help in the music ministry. I work mainly in the music ministry, so I need to find out what gifts are within the ministry and cultivate them. Otherwise, I'd be stuck when it's time to take a vacation because no one else is in place to step in. And I don't want the service to be affected. So, if I provide the opportunity for others to develop their skills, I ease myself out of a job. Now, I no longer have

> **I DON'T GO AHEAD OF OUR PASTOR.**

to be on the praise team. I can just welcome the guests at the end of the praise and worship. I'm also the Community Program Specialist. I found my niche in the community!

Ministries will never be developed if you try to be everything—the secretary, the worship leader, the Sunday school teacher, the Bible study teacher, and the treasurer. Other people will let you do it all. Pray and ask God to show you who can work in the various ministries in the church. That's why First Ladies need to have strong prayer lives. Sometimes this will even enable us to see things that will help our ministries.

Other elect ladies have told me they wish they had trained people earlier on in the ministry. I'm using the word "trained" to imply that everyone is teachable; everyone should be a lifetime learner. One First Lady said, "I wouldn't have had such a hard time motivating them if they were teachable and wanted to learn." Believe it or not; they want to do it your way, but if they had a better idea, would you be open to it? I am a force to be reckoned with when it comes to scheduling and timing. I love people around me who don't procrastinate or sit around and wait to be told what to do. They take the initiative and are movers and shakers. I heard a First Lady say, "If I say I want it tomorrow, I actually want it today." I am not a hard taskmaster at all, I just want everything I do to be done in the spirit of excellence. When we realize it's for God, we should give our best!

Be Careful with God's People

In addition, be careful how you talk to and deal with people. You must always remember they are God's people. They're here to help you. So, be careful how you treat them, speak to them, and show them how to do God's work as the pastor's wife. I knew a pastor's wife who was so mean, I said to myself, "I wouldn't go to that church." I even questioned her one time about it, and she said that people just do what she says. That caught me off guard. Hey! they're not your people; they're God's people, and you must be careful. If they don't do it right or if it's not to your liking, there's a way to say it and there are teachable moments to help and nurture them. People will respond to you and what you need according to how you treat them. Remember, most church work is voluntary. Teach kingdom work and how to win souls and make disciples.

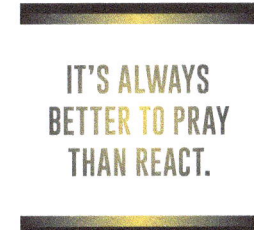

IT'S ALWAYS BETTER TO PRAY THAN REACT.

First Ladies, Can We Talk?

My mother used to say, "When you want to do right, God will help you do right, when you want to be kept, God will keep you." We must always remember that being the pastor's wife often involves spiritual warfare, but it's not our battle. And when we do our part in prayer and fasting, God will do His. My mother also used to say, "Arm yourself likewise."

> Forasmuch then as Christ hath suffered for us in the flesh, arm yourselves likewise with the same mind: for he that hath suffered in the flesh hath ceased from sin.
> (1 Peter 4:1-2 KJV)

Everything we do is to please God. How should we respond to conflicts? I have failed many times by reacting to things because I felt I had the right to say what I wanted to say at that time—and then I ended up apologizing. It's always better to pray than react. I can tell you how to do this because, in the beginning, for the first five years, the struggle was hard. But as the years came and went, I began to discover who God was developing me to be, and that's who I became.

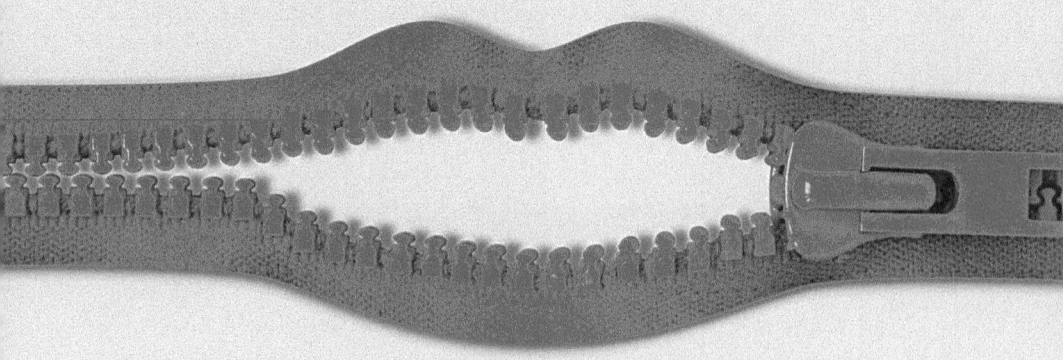

I remember a time we were about to leave church, and someone said something very disrespectful to me. I didn't say anything. When I got home, I said to myself, "So, what just happened?" I got a call later from one of the young members of the church who had witnessed what had happened, letting me know how impressed she was by the way I responded.

"Are you praying and fasting?" she asked.

I said yes! I had been fasting at that particular time because God had told me to fast and pray.

She said, "I could tell."

Fiery Darts

The truth is things don't get to you as the pastor's wife when you stay prayed up and focused on the things that really matter. When you do, you should not be bothered by the things that could tear you up, or make you cry. I promise it will be like water on a duck's back because you are covered in the blood of Jesus. Through prayer and fasting, you miss the fiery darts as it says in Ephesians 6:16:

> Above all, taking the shield of faith with which, you will be able to quench all the fiery darts of the wicked one. (NKJV)

You can say with confidence: "Fiery darts, fiery arrows, I come to destroy your influence."

Those darts are aimed to destroy your self-esteem to make you feel so inadequate that you tell yourself this is not the ministry for you, and you should just go home and never come back. But the shield extinguishes those darts through prayer, faith, and fasting. It's your job and mine to stay watchful and covered. As my mother always says, "Lord, cover me in Your blood, so the Devil can't penetrate me with his fiery arrows and his darts of deceit."

Be encouraged, wife of the pastor! Walk boldly in what God has given you and in the liberty with which Christ has made you free!

I have been both the pastor's wife and the wife of the pastor. Ask God to put you into the hearts of the people. This might sound manipulative, but it's not. Get to know them; get to know their desires, needs, children, and plans. Get to know the people you labor with. Not every First Lady's church can accommodate this. It depends on the size, so wherever you find yourself in ministry ask God which direction you should take.

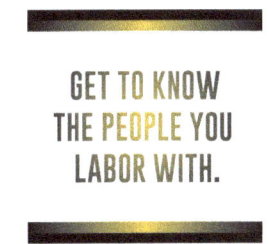

GET TO KNOW THE PEOPLE YOU LABOR WITH.

I'm going to tell a quick story about a First Lady I knew who came into an already established ministry. The pastor's wife had been deceased for several years when he asked for this lady to be his wife. When he was pastoring as a single widow, the church flourished beautifully. The members were loving and caring. They loved their pastor and always wanted to see what they could do for him, and they loved to have him pray for them. Every church has its own dynamics and culture.

So, when the pastor married his new love, it took time for the people to get used to her. They would get up and give accolades to the pastor but not to her, and she would get offended by this. I asked her "Why? They don't know you yet! Let them get to know you; let them fall in love with you first." She would put on different events, but they would not cooperate with her. She asked me what I thought was the reason they weren't cooperating. I told her maybe it was because she was inviting outside people to come in and she was paying them to do what the people in-house could do. That didn't sit well with her.

She would complain, "But they don't like me."

I would say to her, "Have you gotten to know them? Have you invited them to breakfast or lunch and sat down and talked with them to get to know them?"

She said she hadn't. She added that if she didn't like something that was going on in the church, she would get up and walk out.

If I'm honest, as an outsider looking in, I believe her pastor/husband tried everything he could to make her feel wanted and at home and welcomed in the ministry. At the same time, she wanted that position from the start.

Seek Wise Counsel

When my husband began pastoring our ministry, I was already his wife. But there was someone already in place as the Woman's President Coordinator, as well as president of the Missionaries Ministry. I remember talking to my mother about this. When you start ministries or you are a new a pastor's wife, seek wise counsel. Fortunately, I had my mother to talk to who has well over fifty years of experience being a pastor's wife. Whew! She said to me, "Let everybody carry on doing the job they're doing." She added, "A wise woman will sit and watch to see how things are done; take notes and journal, and decide what she wants to do, what she wants to implement, and what she wants to change. But there's no rush to be in that position."

I did just that. I observed the women doing the ministries. I was still the First Lady. As people left, some positions needed to be filled. One of the positions that needed to be filled was called, "The Sisterhood." This was a small in-house convention for the women of the church; it had no formal positions like "missionary" or "evangelist"—they were just laywomen. My mother-in-law suggested that I take this ministry. I went to my pastor and my mother-in-law, and I said, "I will take it if I can change the name and start out fresh the first of the year." They agreed and the Sister-2-Sister Conference was birthed out of it. We are in our seventeenth year to date and God has blessed this ministry.

While my mother-in-law was alive and in charge of the women's ministry as the president, it gave me a chance to observe her to really see how this worked. That allowed me to get to know the women in the ministry, to embrace them and let them embrace and get to know me.

The first year of the conference was not easy because there were people who didn't understand the way I did things. Fortunately, that did not cause us to have any serious fallings-out with one another, apart from an occasional miscommunication glitch. Seventeen years later, because it is an established ministry, I still feel like a pastor's wife. Some would say that should bother me, but it doesn't.

It's through God's grace and kindness that I have also established my own ministry. I am the founder and CEO of a non-profit organization that helps victims of domestic violence called "No Hands Lifted." I have a degree in drug and alcohol and human services. I attended Sacramento Theological Seminary and received a Bachelor of Arts Degree in biblical studies and a master's degree in Christian Counseling, so my mother-in-law occupying that position was a blessing to me. I'm glad I listened to wise counsel. If you are the pastor's wife, ask God why you are in this position.

Referring to the First Lady who wanted to be involved everything... sadly, that church is no longer in existence. I watched her destroy it with her own hands and mouth.

Another First Lady said to me, "I don't want to give him anything or have him do anything for me." She was bitter, and the people could feel her bitterness. Whatever position you find yourself in, whether as the pastor's wife or the wife of the pastor, be wise. Seek counsel with someone who has already walked that path. Pray and ask God. Being kind will preserve you and take you a long way.

A man asked me, "Why do they celebrate the elect ladies?"

I replied, "Why not? If the people want to be kind enough to appreciate them, let them."

Get to know your people because they need to know you. Pretty soon, you'll find God has given you such a glorious life. It's a privilege to be chosen by God to look after His people with the man of God. He chose you to make sure these people get to know who He is through you and prayer and fasting.

Don't Be Disagreeable

Not every First Lady can say she is always in agreement with what her pastor/husband says, and she feels bad about it. But note what Rick Warren said in a sermon about conflict and reconciliation:

> My wife and I are two different people. I have counseled married people that said they were not compatible because they don't think the same. But never forget, people who think the same become too boring. You're not supposed to think the same; you're supposed to have different ways of doing things, different ways of resolving conflict. It's okay to disagree—just don't become disagreeable.

I found as the wife of the pastor, there were times my husband thought I was disagreeing and not complying with him, or not being on his side. However, it was just the opposite. I merely had another way of expressing something that he was trying to convey. Sometimes he would actually admit that I was right. Other times, I would have to balance my opinion and admit he was right. It's okay not to think the same. Some people like to think within the norm; others, by nature, are out-of-the-box thinkers. Either is okay if it works for you.

OUR DIFFERENCES ALLOW US TO WORK WELL TOGETHER.

I am more of a risk-taker than my husband, but he is the one who makes the major business decisions. I'm not afraid to ask for help or to approach someone for what I need. I can reach out to companies and create and send letters to ask for shuttle buses because as the pastor's wife, I know he's covering me. On the other hand, my husband wants to see the end from the beginning first! That being said—our differences allow us to work well together.

A Woman of Grace and Destiny

I remember when I was younger one of my former pastor's wives was a woman of grace and destiny. All the children and young people loved her. One of my favorite memories was how she would take the time to teach us to seek the Lord for ourselves. Even at our age, she didn't want us to be devoured by the Devil. She was talented and played the organ and piano, wrote plays, and did special projects like around-the-world luncheons. She was somebody that everyone could look up to, and she supported her husband.

At the age of twelve, I was at a mid-day prayer service at the church. Our elect lady was on her knees, along with the other women from the church, and when she saw me, she yelled out my name. It scared me because I was not there to pray—I'd come to play with the other children. However, there was something different about the way she called my name. It was with love and authority—now, mind you, she was not a loud overbearing lady; rather, she was soft-spoken and easy to entreat. But I heard a different sound in her voice: "Leisa, come here quick! The Lord wants to fill you with the Holy Ghost!" I believed her without a doubt. Tears started to fall from my face. I lifted my hands with a pure heart and was filled with the Holy Spirit.

I not only loved and respected my elect lady, but I also observed a few things about her. There were women in our church who would disrespect her and talk down to her. However, I never saw her react. I saw her do what the Bible instructed us to do in Matthew Chapter 5, the beatitudes, "Do good to those who despitefully use you and say all manner of evil against you falsely." I would hear her in prayer believing God to work on her behalf. And He turned everything around for her.

I encourage you with 1 Corinthians 15:58:

> Therefore, my dear brothers and sisters, stand firm. Let nothing move you. Always give yourselves fully to the work of the Lord, because you know that your labor in the Lord is not in vain (NIV).

And so, I give a shout-out to all these wonderful First Ladies I have been blessed to know. But the prime First Lady I speak of is my mother! Lady Rochelle Wynn Anderson. When my father passed, she remarried and is still an elect lady. Her steps may not be as long, and her eyes may be a little dim, but her wonderful and caring ways have not changed. We often share and exchange information to help the women in our ministries. She's still as strong in her mind as she was when I was a child. She was anointed to do what she is still doing. I salute you, Mom. I honor you, and I hope I can make you proud of me. You are the real deal: Pastor's Wife/Elect Lady Rochelle Wynn-Anderson!

PRAYER

Father, I thank You for Your amazing Word that has transformed us to be smarter and better women. We will please You, Father. We aim to be who Your Word declares we should be. You have fashioned and made us women of God. We are respected and loved by You. Father, we thank You for Your love and concern. We are gifts to our spouses as they are gifts to the body of Christ. Thank You, Lord, for Your Spirit that dwells in us. Together, we are a ministry. In Jesus' name, Amen.

WRITE YOUR AFFIRMATION OF RESPECT AND LOVE

CONCLUSION

Now all has been heard; here is the conclusion of the matter: Fear God and keep his commandments, for this is the duty of all mankind. (Ecclesiastes 12:13 NIV)

The year 1992 was an eye-opener for me. The only thing I had under my belt was cosmetology and I was certified in phlebotomy, but I had no idea how to write a check or open a bank account. My sister Karen taught me how to do things I didn't know how to do. Thank you, so much Karen for loving and teaching me. I allowed my unhealthy past relationship to dictate my goals and my future, and blind me to my worth and capabilities.

I learned that no matter how much you love, care, and help, you must learn how to be resourceful. As women, we can think and handle tasks simultaneously without allowing them to distract us. In other words, we can multitask. This was the year I found out that depending on any one person was not enough. The only one we should fully depend on is God or the people He sends into our lives. Now, don't get me wrong. I'm not saying there aren't some marriage relationships that are strong and complete with the sole provider being the husband.

WAIT ON GOD FOR YOUR HUSBAND!

When my children and I moved back to California in 1992, my life began to change. I knew as a woman I had to learn and know more to go further in life, and I desired more. I longed for more. Because of my past experiences and not knowing and being unwise, I no longer wanted to be that person. I was what I call an independent dependent. In my past relationship, I wasn't allowed to think or function without permission. Sisters, hear me. Wait on God for your husband! Sometimes we don't want to wait, and we marry wrong— all wrong. I declare that you will wait on God.

I praise God for my godly husband, Pastor Harold Johnson II, who allows me to be me and supports me. He loves me beyond me. Although my past experiences were painful, they made me strong! They made me a better person. I took all the past experiences and coupled them with my new beginning, and it has catapulted me to become a powerful, strong woman.

I refused to be a victim, and I became resourceful. I didn't know how resourceful I was in this position as an elect lady. Every tool and resource I have up to now has helped me to thrive. First Lady, we can do this! I pray that God grants you the ability to be all He has made you to be. Ask God to reveal to you what He desires from you. God has amazing plans for your life. Even when we can't see, He is our bright light. He is a compass and our engineer.

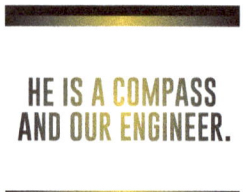

HE IS A COMPASS AND OUR ENGINEER.

Keep On Pressing

Remember to make prayer your portion. I promise you; it is the only way I have made it thus far. In 2012 my sisters and I, along with my mom, started praying every morning at 5:00 a.m. Yes, it is a sacrifice. A lot of mornings I didn't feel like getting up. But, I found the secret to God was through prayer; this is where God would reveal Himself to me. I would get His full attention. I also have His ear during worship.

I began to study the art of praying, for lack of a better word. When I would get down on my knees, distractions and mind chatter would always meet me. But First Lady, keep pressing. Yes, it is a press. I will call that the first realm. The more I began to pray through, the distractions didn't seem as overwhelming. However, this is when I started to think I was unworthy. This is the plan of satan to keep you from prayer. How could I even ask a great big God to look into my problem? I will call this the second realm. My sister, I kept right on pressing. Then, I got to the realm where I no longer cared about anything but giving God His glory, praise, and honor. Prayer, First Lady, is like putting money in a savings account; the more you do it, the more you have stored up. Prayers stored are used in times when you can't pray for yourself.

One particular morning, I know it was a Tuesday because that's my day. I was in my prayer room—yes, First Lady, I have a prayer room. This is a blessed room; when it gets cluttered, I clean it because this is where I meet God. The room is painted a light beige with a nice bed, carpeted floor, and a chair to kneel at if I choose to do so. I was on my knees. I had been praying for about twenty minutes. I was praying for the people of God and their healing. I was not just praying for our four and no more; I cried out for the women, men, and children of God. It was an unusually cold morning. I had a blanket around my shoulders; it was in late November. I prayed and began to speak in my heavenly language, and I felt a cool wind blowing over my head while still praying; I looked up and thought to myself, "Did my husband turn on the air?" Then it stopped just as quickly as it started. I started to pray even more earnestly when I felt a whooshing feeling of air brush over me again. This time, it was stronger. I stopped immediately. I knew at that moment what I was experiencing was beyond me. I ended the prayer. I said nothing to my sister or my mom. I got out of the prayer room. Let me be a little transparent… I was afraid.

I walked into my bedroom where my husband was. By this time, he was getting ready for work. When he left for work, I called my friend Norris. I needed him to answer me like the Prophet he was. I began to explain to him what happened in prayer that morning; he chuckled and said in a sarcastic way, "Girl, you know what that was? It was an angel." I hung up and said to myself let me call my brother.

I called Bishop John Wynn, my brother who stayed on his face in prayer. I told myself he would have a different answer. When I told Bishop my experience, he asked me in a quiet, calm voice, "Do you remember what you were praying for?" I answered him, "Yes, I was praying for healing." He laughed and said you were praying, and I believe the angel Raphael, the healing angel, came for your words. Then, he threw me a curveball when he said, "Did you tell your husband?" I said no and he said to tell him because he experienced it also.

When my husband got home, I told him about my morning experience; he didn't laugh nor chuckle. He asked me a question, "Babe, this morning when you were praying, I heard you louder than usual. It was like the presence of the Lord was throughout the whole house. While you were praying before you finished, did you step out of the prayer room?" I answered, "No. Why?" He looked me in my face and said I could still hear you praying, but our bedroom door opened. All I saw was a flash of light then the door closed back rapidly. I believe I had a visitation and the wind I felt was his wings. Apostle Hillard said, "My experience is never at the mercy of another person's argument." It's not up for debate or doubt as far as I'm concerned.

This book is about you, my sister, First Lady. It is in God we live, move, and have our being. We are not superwomen, but when we love to pray and serve the God of the Bible, He adds super to our natural. Really get to know God in truth:

> But the people that do know their God shall be strong, and do exploits. (Daniel 11:32b)

God knows our end from the beginning. God knows what is best for our lives. I encourage you to trust Him and lean not to your own understanding. He sees you and will always be there for you. At the end of the day, we must please God. If our great God positioned, you here, you've got this! The Word of God declares that there is nothing too hard for God. The goal is to love in spite of. First Lady, do your part from your heart. Let your motives be pure. Be resilient; be resourceful. I see you, First Lady! You are stronger than you think. Be great in God. God honors a pure heart. We may not know it all, but we know God knows all things. First Lady, can we talk? God is always listening.

PRAYER

Lord, I thank you for the conclusion of the whole matter. Let everyone that reads this book find a word or phrase that leads them to their place of clam. Help my sister to accept what God has allowed. May God grant you your secret desires as you walk out this journey with grace, peace and love. I'm praying for you daily. In Jesus' name. Amen.

WRITE YOUR AFFIRMATION OF VICTORY

_____
_____
_____
_____
_____
_____
_____
_____
_____
_____

ACKNOWLEDGMENTS

First, to my husband, I'm here because you answered the call. We have been a close working team to do this. You told me years ago that you have studied me to see what makes me tick, and you have supported me for over twenty-five years as I continue to be who God has designed me to be. Love you!

To all eight of our children, Elliot aka "Marcus," Jhamond, Kristopher aka "Kross," Cherael aka "Coco Ja," Briane, Tyler, Isaiah, and Chara aka "LaLa," Mommy loves you to life. You let me practice being a First Lady on you. To Jaya our bonus daughter it has been a privilege to help your mother raise you. Wow since the age of five, you've been a part of all of us. To Siobhan, my daughter-in-love, watch close. Tag! You are next in line for purpose. Believe what I say.

I have been fortunate to have First Ladies in my life who saw something in me before I saw the good in myself. My very first, First Lady was my mother. You've operated with such grace and poise, even to this day. You've counted it as a privilege to serve the people of God. A close friend of mine calls you "Mother Grace" because you carry yourself and operate like a modern-day Kathryn Kuhlman.

I had the privilege of being your First Lady and you have never blurred the lines navigating between your daughter and First Lady.

My forever mother-in-love, First Lady Barbra Jean Brown, you taught me to take a licking and keep on ticking. You would often say, "Don't be no wimp!" Even through sickness, you taught me to trust God and believe in His sovereignty. There are so many pastors' wives you birthed by your example.

I want to thank every pastor's wife who has had a part in my journey. Lady Vicki L Kemp, thank you for the hours you took looking over my baby, yes, this book! Your expertise and the knowledge you've shared on how to get this book to the world have been invaluable. Thank you also for your book coaching and consulting.

Thank you, Lady Rita Edwards, for the benefit of your calm nature and wisdom—like Abigail; I learned to cope with obstacles. Lady Phyllis Thomas, I'm grateful for your continued reminder that prayer still works! And Lady Renee Allen, the secret keeper, who every lady needs, I'm indebted to you. To all my sisters who at one time were all walking in the calling of the First Lady, I have learned so much from all of you. Pastor Patricia Wynn Tau, you were the first one to be a pastor's wife, and you taught me the art of silence, even when you're right. Now that role has fallen on me. I salute you!

Pastor Robbye Wynn-Nicholson, I learned how to work in the marketplace doing conferences from you. You taught me that no matter how great our ideas may be, to always rely on the power of God, never our own strength. Sweet Lady, Karen Wynn-Allen, and Lady Sharon Wynn, you have hearts of gold, and I would not be where I am without your continued prayers and support. You have both walked in this calling, thank you for your perspectives. Bishop William John Wynn, you have always believed in my abilities and pushed me to greater heights. I will always be your Baptist preacher. Wilhelmina Wynn and Juanita Wynn, I love you both—we are family. There's one thing I know for sure: we have each other's back.

Special thanks to Lady Janet aka Elaine Bronson. You saved my life when I didn't recognize I needed to be saved over thirty-five years ago. Much love and respect. To Evangelist Kimberly Day-Williams and Lady Denise Slaughter, thank you for your continued support. To Mother Carolyn Galbraith, thank you for your continued wisdom and prayers. To Mother Mary Johnson, thank you for giving me my wonderful husband.

Thank you to Christian Living Books, Inc. for your incredible work in bringing my vision to life. Your expertise is amazing. I thank you so much for producing my gift to First Ladies.

Finally, to The Path, our church family, it has been my pleasure to be your First Lady. Because of your love and support for me and my family, I enjoyed doing what we have been called to do. Even through the pandemic you all were consistent in giving your time, your dime, and your talent. I understand that church members choose where they worship and I'm glad you chose me. Smooches.

ABOUT THE AUTHOR

Evangelist Leisa Wynn-Johnson is a vessel being used by God to impact the lives of His people. She accepted the call to minister the Word of God as a young adult while serving under the pastorate of her parents, the late Rev. W.J. Wynn, and her mother, Rochelle Wynn. She is the wife of Supt. Harold Johnson, II, and serves in numerous capacities at her local church, including Women's Department President and Community Program Administrator. She is known as a working First Lady because she willingly and diligently labors wherever there is a need.

Evangelist Wynn-Johnson has a passion for outreach and a gift for connecting with people and winning them into the Kingdom. Her outreach style, much like her speaking style, is down-to-earth, practical, and engaging, granting her broad appeal to people from all walks of life. A large part of her outreach focus is on women who have experienced various traumas in life. Armed with a powerful testimony of her personal experience of God's power, she has been graced to mentor and help rebuild hurting women.

She is the coordinator of the annual Sister-2-Sister Conference, which sponsors charitable outreach to victims of domestic violence, as well as displaced and impoverished families. She is also the CEO of No Hands Lifted, a non-profit organization that collaborates with Sister-2-Sister to serve women and families in the community, providing resources, clothing, supplies, and meals at various times of the year. She is the mother of eight children who assist in the ministry in various capacities.

Evangelist Wynn-Johnson attended Sacramento Theological Seminary, where she earned a Bachelor of Arts Degree in Biblical Studies and a Master's Degree in Christian Counseling. Evangelist Wynn-Johnson is the author of the book, *The Many Faces of Domestic Violence*. She recently earned her Associate of Science degree in Addiction Studies and Humanities. Her focus and the driving force in her ministry is that, when all is said and done, only what we do for Christ will last.

Connect with the Author

- LeisaWynnJohnsonMinistry@gmail.com
- LeisaWynn-Johnson.com
- IamLeisaWynnJohn_
- Leisa Wynn-Johnson

www.ingramcontent.com/pod-product-compliance
Lightning Source LLC
Chambersburg PA
CBHW040304170426
43194CB00021B/2888